DOING BRIEF PSYCHOTHERAPY

DOING BRIEF
PSYCHOTHERAPY

MICHAEL FRANZ BASCH

BasicBooks
A Subsidiary of Perseus Books, L.L.C.

Library of Congress Cataloging-in-Publication Data
Basch, Michael Franz
    Doing brief psychotherapy / by Michael Franz Basch.
    p.   cm.
    Includes bibliographical references and index.
    ISBN 0–465–09548–8
    1. Brief psychotherapy.   2. Brief psychotherapy—Case studies.   I. Title.
    [DNLM: 1. Psychotherapy, Brief—methods—case studies.   WM
420.5.P5 B289d   1995]
RC480.55.B37   1995
616.89'14—dc20
DNLM/DLC
for Library of Congress   95–18429
                                                                      CIP

98 ❖/HC 9 8 7 6 5 4

To

Erik Thomas Basch

October 5, 1994

Bon Voyage

CONTENTS

List of Illustrations   ix
Preface   xi
Acknowledgments   xvii
Introduction   xxi

PART I: THE DEVELOPMENTAL MODEL

Chapter 1.   *Setting a Goal and Focusing*
                 the Treatment: Denise Taft   3

Chapter 2.   *Restoring Competence: Ralph Jerome*   18

PART II: BRIEF PSYCHOTHERAPY AND THE
                 GOAL OF CHARACTER CHANGE

Chapter 3.   *The Patient as an*
                 Agent for Change: Bea Willingham   37

Chapter 4.   *Correcting a Developmental Deficit:*
                 Warren Dale, Jr.   54

Chapter 5.   *Shame and the Restoration*
                 of Self-Esteem: Jacob Cain   77

Chapter 6.   *Validating a Change: Franklin Furlong*   102

Chapter 7.   *When More Time Is Needed to Achieve Character Change: Michelle Longwood*   120

PART III.   BRIEF PSYCHOTHERAPY AND LIMITED GOALS

Chapter 8.   *Clarification and Guidance: Grant Rausen and William Semic*   131

Chapter 9.   *Restoring the Status Quo: Nadine Nelson and Gerald Shellman*   162

Chapter 10.   *Problem Solving: Roger Povalente*   169

References   177
Index   183

LIST OF ILLUSTRATIONS

Figure 1.1   Sectors of Development
Figure 1.2   The Developmental Spiral
Figure 1.3   A Guide to Problem-Solving Intervention
Figure 2.1   Ranges of Basic Affect
Figure 2.2   The Positive Transference

PREFACE

B RIEF PSYCHOTHERAPY—treatment concluded in no more than twenty sessions—is often seen as a compromise. During the training of the dynamic psychotherapist, the idea becomes firmly imprinted that longer is better. Experience has taught me, however, that shorter is anything but second-best. In a majority of cases, short-term treatment, effectively applied, enables the patient to reach the same therapeutic goals as long-term psychotherapy, while offering the added advantage of relieving the patient's psychic stress that much sooner. Moreover, I believe that one cannot decide arbitrarily, on the basis of either symptoms or character structure, that a patient will not benefit from brief therapy. Indeed, it is my position that all patients who are not psychotic or suicidal should be thought of as candidates for brief psychotherapy until proven otherwise.

At first blush it may seem odd for a card-carrying psychoanalyst to be writing about short-term treatment. But I am not suggesting that brief psychotherapy is a substitute for either psychoanalysis or open-ended psychotherapy. The point is simply that very few of the people referred to me for treatment need such extensive therapy. More often than not, patients and I work together for a while, come to a reasonable resolution of their respective difficulties, and part company. Pleased as I am for them when they depart, I do occasionally grumble that no one sends me real, honest-to-goodness psychoanalytic treatment cases anymore. I thought I was just doing my job, but it turns out that all this time I have been doing brief psychotherapy.

I learned that this was the case when distressed colleagues and students complained to me in seminars and supervisory sessions that restrictions imposed upon them by third-party payers made it no longer possible to do decent work. It seemed that many of their patients were literally in tears, begging for a chance to talk with a therapist rather than simply having their medications adjusted, but the consensus among the clinicians was that their restricted access to psychiatric services made it impossible to start any kind of psychotherapy. After all, what could one hope to accomplish when access to the patient was arbitrarily limited at the outset? Plenty, I thought, when I heard the cases presented. I would have been happy to work with them within the imposed time limits.

It did not take me long to identify the problem that stood in the way of delivering appropriate care to these patients. Prepared only to approach every patient with the model Freud developed for treating psychoneurotic patients—a therapeutic technique that involves a lengthy exploration of childhood—these therapists were stymied when open-ended therapy was not an option.

As the saying goes, when all you have is a hammer, everything looks like a nail. I have been fortunate enough to have had a few psychoneurotic patients, with whom the psychoanalytic hammer works just fine. We drive the nail as deep as it will go—that is, through the patient's defenses and all the way down to those early memories and fantasies that the patient would give anything not to have to look at, much less recognize and call by name. But why pound away at those poor patients whose problem is written on their foreheads, who are not resistant to coming to know what they need to know, and whose capacity for salutary change does not depend on uncovering deeply buried secrets?

My own experience, as well as that of my students and supervisees, has demonstrated that therapy is often prolonged not because of the patient's need but because the therapist does not know how and where to intervene. I am well aware that we all have hidden issues that in principle are only discoverable through a psychoanalytically oriented exploration of early childhood, but does it follow that that is the route all psychotherapy must take? That would make about as much sense as deciding that since insulin is life-saving for diabetic patients, and since we all have a pancreas, insulin is the treatment for all bodily ailments.

Since Freud first formulated his theory and technique, much has been learned about normal psychological development and attachment. This knowledge, translated into practical technique, forms the basis of a new, though still dynamic, therapeutic approach that I call the *developmental model*. In brief, developmental psychotherapy locates the patient's problem in one or another area in which development appears to have been impaired and at the same time takes account of those areas in which the patient is functioning, or capable of functioning, productively. Thus it avoids unnecessary regression and prolonged therapy by beginning with the working assumption that the patient possesses the resources to cope with problems and that it is the therapist's job to mobilize these resources to good effect. In other words, I see the patient not simply as a victim of the past but as an agent for change in the present.

By working with their assets in this manner, patients can reach reasonable goals in a reasonable amount of time. For many patients, brief therapy opens the way to basic and lasting character change. For others, brief therapy is effective in resolving a particular problem that impairs or threatens to undo a functional psychological adaptation. For those who do require longer treatment, brief psychotherapy serves as a diagnostic evaluation that clarifies the situation and provides an opportunity to discuss the need for other modes of therapy and the options open to them.

This book describes the developmental model of brief psychotherapy, using case histories as matrices from which to extract guidelines for technique that are based on normal development. Readers who are acquainted with the literature on brief psychotherapy will be quick to see that my approach is quite different from other models of treatment, which for the most part still rely on the psychoanalytic exploration of unconscious oedipal conflict. What I am proposing, however, is inclusive, not exclusive; the contributions of Franz Alexander, Habib Davanloo, David Malan, James Mann, and Peter Sifneos, among others, can be explained by and in turn be used to enhance developmental psychotherapy. In the introductory chapter, I review the four models of brief dynamic psychotherapy most often referred to in the literature today. These models have in common a number of aspects of technique that should be retained, even as we formulate an approach that avoids their limitations.

The first part of the book outlines the developmental model in clinical context. I use here two cases presented to me by residents in clinical seminars to demonstrate how one can avoid the trap of regression by identifying the aspects of development in which the patient has strengths, so that those strengths can be used to correct the failed development in other areas that has led to counterproductive strategies. The second section of the book elaborates the model, using as case material patients from my own practice who lent themselves to a proactive therapeutic stance and experienced significant character change. At the end of this section, I identify and discuss those clinical situations that are not suitable for the short-term approach and describe why some patients require lengthier treatment to achieve such a character change. The treatments of a variety of difficult—and initially discouraging—patients make up the third and final section of the book. These people illustrate how one can achieve meaningful, albeit limited, results in cases that could easily have been given up as hopeless or, alternatively, could well have dragged on in therapy without ever coming to therapeutic closure.

Since ideal patients are found more often in textbooks than in one's practice, I have purposely chosen to present case examples that do not fall within the narrow parameters of acceptability advocated by various other schools of short-term treatment. The reader will find me illustrating the application of the developmental model with a mixture of what, at least initially, look like not-so-great, challenging cases—the patients that are typically encountered by any of us who have an office, a telephone, and open hours in our schedule.

Of course, case histories or composites have been sufficiently altered to prevent identification of any individual patient. I have retained an accurate description of the therapeutic interchange, however, in order to spell out the how, why, and when of the technique that I advocate. Too often clinical protocols demonstrate the skill of the therapist conducting the treatment but leave the reader wondering how principles were transformed into particular interventions. I have attempted to forestall such frustration by describing, step by step, how my interventions were derived. In this way I hope to illustrate the developmental rationale for a particular move with a given patient without tying the developmental model to a technique that suits my personality but not necessarily another's. My aim is to formulate an approach to psychotherapy that is prescriptive without being either so general that it is useless, or so specific that it is idiosyncratic.

Since the book deals primarily with psychotherapeutic technique, I have kept theoretical discussions to a minimum and presented the developmental model and its application as succinctly as possible. Elsewhere, however, I have detailed the background and the justification for the clinical principles that are proposed here more or less dogmatically (Basch 1988, 1992).

Most therapists seem to expect that achieving meaningful change in treatment is of necessity slow, difficult, and convoluted. It need not be so. The model for therapy that I advocate is straightforward and accessible, and it works. Length of experience in the field is not the issue. I have been encouraged by the success of my beginning students, once I have persuaded them that gray hair is not a prerequisite for learning to use the developmental model. Many of them attain, in a matter of a few weeks or months, a level of therapeutic expertise that in years past I could hope to see them achieve only in a decade of practice, if ever.

I hope that what I have written will have something to say to teachers, students, and practitioners alike. My goal has been to write a book usable by therapists of all persuasions, not only psychoanalytically oriented practitioners like me, whose training did not prepare us for a climate in which the demands are great and the options are few, but all therapists who find the constraints of time limits frustrating. With a model such as the developmental model proposed here, we no longer need consider these constraints as detrimental to the therapeutic process.

ACKNOWLEDGMENTS

Once AGAIN, I am happy to express my thanks to Jan Fawcett, M.D., chairman of the Department of Psychiatry, Rush Medical College, who suggested that this book was needed, convinced me to write it, and afforded me the time to complete it.

When a readable draft had taken shape, I rounded up the usual suspects and all went over the manuscript through its many revisions until it was at last in the publisher's hands. I am much indebted to Robert Buchanan, M.D., Roy R. Grinker, Jr., M.D., Paul C. Holinger, M.D., Charles M. Jaffe, M.D., Gary Rosenmutter, M.D., and Virginia C. Saft, M.D., whose suggestions and emendations helped me tremendously. Their support and companionship made the task ever so much lighter and more enjoyable than it would have been otherwise.

Additionally, good friends and colleagues took the time and trouble to read the penultimate draft of the book with great care. I benefited immeasurably from the comments regarding both content and style that I received from Douglas Detrick, Ph.D., Miriam Elson, M.A., A.C.S.W., Richard Gardiner, M.D., Jill R. Gardner, Ph.D., Arnold Goldberg, M.D., Constance Goldberg, M.S.W., David E. Morrison, M.D., and Donald L. Nathanson, M.D.

The comments on various specific aspects of the manuscript by Gail Basch, M.D., Stephanie Cavenaugh, M.D., Suzanne Cooperman,

M.D., Peter Fink, M.D., Karen Pierce, M.D., and Abbie Sivan, Ph.D., are also very much appreciated. I am once again grateful to Beatrice Beebe, Ph.D., for clarifying a number of issues for me in the area of infant development.

In the classroom, the resident physicians in psychiatry at Rush Medical College gave me excellent feedback as I used the developmental model to teach psychotherapeutic technique. All were helpful, and I thank them collectively. For the contributions of John Heather, M.D., I owe a particular debt of gratitude, and I acknowledge it with pleasure.

Thanks to Gilbert Levin, Ph.D., director of the Cape Cod Institute, I was able to present my thoughts about brief psychotherapy at the Institute, which is sponsored yearly by the Department of Psychiatry of the Albert Einstein College of Medicine. As in my previous presentations to this seminar, the opportunity to exchange ideas with colleagues from all areas of the country, as well as from foreign shores, was exhilarating, educational, and much appreciated.

Mrs. Therese Molyneux, administrative secretary in the Department of Psychiatry of Rush Medical College, made my task much easier by relieving me of the innumerable logistic details involved in preparing the various versions of the manuscript for distribution. Many thanks.

As she always has done before, Jo Ann Miller, vice president of Basic Books, encouraged, supported, and advised me throughout. Her efforts on my behalf are much appreciated.

It was my good fortune to have Nina Gunzenhauser edit the manuscript. Her suggestions—lexical, syntactic, and stylistic—invariably left me with the reaction "Yes, *that's* what I wanted to say." Many, many thanks.

This being our fourth book together, I am running out of words and phrases with which to acknowledge Eva Sandberg's invaluable contribution to these endeavors. Readers who see the adult version, so to speak, have not had to participate, as Eva has, in raising this volume from its babyhood. As it grew, page by page, revision upon revision, Eva not only bore with me and gave my ideas typewritten form but on occasion made comments and suggestions that steered me in the right direction. As she knows by now, the reward for her good work will be more work; I have no doubt that Eva and I will shortly be heading down this road again. I could not want a better comrade.

Having written gives me pleasure, but writing does not always do so by any means. No one knows this better than my wife. Carol cheers me on when the writing is going well and cheers me up when it is not. Her confidence that I not only can but will do what I feel I must sustained me and let an idea become a reality.

INTRODUCTION

E VER SINCE FREUD demonstrated that the incapacitating symptoms of psychoneuroses could be cured through analysis of the oedipal trauma of childhood, his approach has been adopted as the gold standard for all dynamic psychotherapy in general (Goldberg 1995). The time, effort, and expense required for a psychoanalysis, however, as well as the limited number of fully trained psychoanalysts, soon led to efforts to make Freud's insights available to greater numbers of emotionally troubled people. It was hoped that the psychoanalytic method could be modified so that the therapy would be less demanding but would still obtain a cure based on an understanding of the childhood origin of the patient's difficulty. So began what is called *psychoanalytically oriented, dynamic,* or *insight psychotherapy.*

Although patients seen in dynamic psychotherapy had fewer sessions per week than patients in analysis, so that the time and the expense required for treatment were reduced, the length of the therapy, like that of psychoanalysis, was still measured in years. As the demand and need for short-term psychotherapy grew, various models were developed in the hope that one might be able to reach a psychoanalytic goal in a shorter period of time.

The brief psychotherapies of Habib Davanloo (1980), David Malan (1976), James Mann (1973), and Peter Sifneos (1992), the best-known examples of this genre, all adhere to an oedipal explanation of psychopathology. Only in method do these therapies depart the traditional model. Whereas the analyst—or the psychotherapist practicing an open-ended kind of therapy—takes a seemingly passive attitude toward the patient, letting the latter's story unfold as much as possible under its own steam, the practitioners of brief treatment advocate an active, aggressive attitude on the part of the therapist. All make the assumption that though the patient's focal conflict may be hidden (repressed) from the patient, that conflict is evident to the trained observer who takes a detailed history. Once the patient's presumed basic conflict has been brought into focus, the therapist pursues it relentlessly. As the various cases described illustrate, the therapist challenges the patient whenever the latter seems to want to evade what the therapist has concluded is the oedipally related issue, especially if the patient gives signs of wanting to take a dependent, regressive position. Every effort is made to bring the conflict into the transference, so as to confront the patient with this repetition in the here and now of the therapeutic situation (Budman 1981; Crits-Christoph & Barber 1991; Flegenheimer 1982; Zeig & Gilligan 1990).

A common feature of traditional psychoanalysis and these brief psychotherapies is that they are all anxiety-provoking. In an analysis the analyst, in the interest of reaching deeper levels of motivation, raises the patient's anxiety by withholding the usual communications with which people signal acceptance, understanding, and safety. As the clinical illustrations in support of the above-mentioned brief psychotherapies show, the therapist then provokes intense anxiety by adamantly pursuing the "secret" the patient is harboring but refusing to acknowledge. Ideally, under the pressure of increasing anxiety, the patient faces what has been avoided and is rewarded not only by newfound insight but by the implicit approval of the therapist, who now behaves in collegial rather than adversarial fashion. The patient's initially self-defeating behavior has usually benefited, often dramatically, from the ongoing interchange with the therapist, and both have every reason to be pleased by the outcome.

My reading of the cases adduced in these models, however, suggests to me that the problems successfully treated by these clinicians are not problems of neurotic guilt—that is, difficulties stemming from unresolved oedipal conflicts that have been inadequately repressed (Basch 1988). Generally, the cases cited are of patients who seek therapy to deal with various problems in forming or maintaining relationships. As these patients' histories reveal, they either suffered abusive overstimulation in childhood or, at the opposite end of the spectrum, experienced vicious rejection of their longings for affection. As a result of either form of assault on their early affective development, they carried a sense of shame and worthlessness into their adult lives, a lack of self-esteem that led to the presenting difficulty. In these cases the therapists are not dealing with unconscious memories but, quite the contrary, with vivid ones, which the patients are doing their best to sequester. Only when the therapist forced the articulation of these memories were the patients able to make a connection between those only-too-well-remembered traumatic insults and their symptomatology. Effective as these therapies may have been for the patients involved, they do not meet the claim that they serve to unearth problems of infantile sexuality and resolve repressed oedipal issues. Therefore, they do not support the assertion that short-term treatment can accomplish what can be done through psychoanalysis or open-ended psychotherapy when such treatment is indicated.

The founders of these schools of brief psychotherapy present ample, detailed case material and follow-up studies that attest to the profound and lasting effect of their respective therapies, and we have no reason to doubt that what they have done worked well for the patients described. The problem with these therapies is that they have extremely limited usefulness because of the demands they make on the treatment situation, the patient, and the therapist. These methods have been developed in academic research settings in which a careful screening process takes place before a patient is selected for such anxiety-provoking therapy. Patients who are not accepted can be cared for in other parts of the clinic, and those who have begun treatment but for one reason or another drop out, become too disturbed to continue, or are judged to be treatment failures can switch to a different form of therapy. Desirable as such resources are, most therapists do not practice where these options are available to their patients.

The patient usually described as suitable for these therapies has a circumscribed problem, preferably of recent origin, and has a history of at least some satisfying childhood relationships. The person has reasonable expectations of therapy and the therapist, is insightful and emotionally self-aware, and can make and adhere to a therapeutic contract (Burke, White, & Havens 1979; Flegenheimer 1982; Gustafson 1984; Strupp 1980a, 1980b, 1980c). In other words, the suitable patient according to these models of brief therapy is that ideal patient whom we all hope for but seldom see (Lazarus & Fay 1990). Not surprisingly, therefore, only a small number of patients have both a suitable problem and the strength to withstand and benefit from the anxiety-provoking confrontation to which they are subjected in these forms of brief therapy. The percentage of patients screened and accepted (but not necessarily successfully treated) for these short-term treatments is given variously as between 3 percent and 23 percent (Flegenheimer 1982; Lazarus & Fay 1990).

What is usually not mentioned but becomes immediately clear when one reads the case illustrations is that even with a paragon for a patient the therapist would have to be very experienced and highly skilled to achieve the promised results. In the case material there is no clarification of the technique that the therapist used to identify, isolate, and refine the problem on which the patient is to be focused and on which everything depends; it is taken as a given. (James Mann [1981], the founder of Time-Limited Psychotherapy, is the exception; he specifically states that those who wish to use his method should be experienced in long-term psychotherapy and have themselves had personal treatment, preferably psychoanalysis.) Additionally, given the brief and intense nature of the work, the therapist is variously admonished to be totally neutral, totally accepting of the patient, totally attuned to the patient, totally empathic with the patient; there seems to be no room for error. How many of us would care or dare to assume that mantle of perfection?

I think of my approach as the mirror image of those just discussed. I consider all patients, with the exception of those who are psychotic or suicidal, to be suitable for a trial of brief developmental psychotherapy. In other words, every patient is expected to be a brief psychotherapy patient until the course of the treatment demonstrates that a different approach is called for.

I do not try to bring about the patient's compliance by creating a high level of stress. The great majority of patients I encounter are already in the grips of anxiety; my goal is to use my knowledge of development to understand why that is so, to reduce or eliminate anxiety as quickly as possible, and to do what I can to prepare the patient to cope more effectively if and when the occasion arises again.

I do not require that a patient exhibit near-to-ideal psychological wherewithal; on the contrary, I consider it my job to elicit and foster the patient's strengths. I share the afore-mentioned colleagues' emphasis on the therapist's active, assertive, goal-directed stance, but I do not go out of my way to force what I believe to be the patient's problem into the relationship with me. My focus is not primarily on the origins of the patient's difficulties in childhood but on the reasons why the strengths the patient has developed no longer serve and what if anything I might be able to do to rectify that situation.

Although my approach is dynamic in the sense of relying on the primacy of unconscious thought and the transference of patterns of expectation, it does not depend on the oedipal conflict for an explanation of all psychopathology. To the contrary, the resolution of an oedipal conflict, as Freud learned from experience, necessitates a lengthy and convoluted undoing of unconscious defenses behind which lies the source of the patient's difficulties—in other words, a psychoanalysis. If it turns out that an oedipal conflict is central to a patient's problem, the patient must be told why a psychoanalytic approach is required and brief therapy must be brought to a close once the patient has had a chance to deal with whatever anxiety attends that recommendation. A similar caveat holds for patients who have deep-seated narcissistic personality disorders (Basch 1988; Goldberg 1973). The patients requiring open-ended or psychoanalytic therapy are, however, in the minority.

It is the lack of a viable alternative to the oedipal theory of development that has hampered the development of a broadly applicable dynamic approach to short-term treatment. This problem has now been resolved. In the last fifty years or so, much has been learned about normal development through infant research. Important as the oedipal conflict is for the psychoneurotic patient, it is only one component of a much broader developmental process (Basch 1988, 1992; Karen 1994; Stern 1985, 1989, 1990). Similarly, the work of Silvan Tomkins (1970, 1980, 1981; Nathanson 1987, 1992) in the realm of affect theory has enhanced our knowledge of development and human motivation. Addressing the issue of development from the clinical side, the work of the psychoanalyst Heinz Kohut (1971, 1977, 1984, 1987; Basch 1986) has extended our understanding of attachment problems and the therapeutic significance of the positive transference. Freud's work emphasized the negative transference, the transference to the analyst of what was hidden from and abhorrent to the patient (1912a, 1912b, 1913, 1914, 1915). For Freud, the nonerotic positive transference, which he called the ally of the analyst, was taken for granted and not further examined. Kohut's work dissected the positive transference in patients with attachment disorders into its components and showed its importance not only for therapy but for development generally. It is the concept of what Kohut (1984) called the *selfobject* that makes possible a bridge between normal development and the treatment process. *Selfobject* is Kohut's neologism and is based on the infant/mother relationship, in which for the first eighteen months or so the baby does not conceptualize the mother as a person in her own right but simply as an extension of the needy self (Kohut 1971, 1984).

Kohut's recognition that the danger to a cohesive self organization comes from more than oedipal frustration led him to postulate three basic needs that are with us from the beginning to the end of life and whose significant frustration at any time in the life cycle may give rise to psychopathology. In essence, he was saying that it is these more basic needs, rather than sexuality and aggression per se, that are the basic motivators for behavior. Designating these needs by the manner in which they show up in therapy, he labeled them the *alter ego* or *twinship transference,* the *idealizing transference,* and the *mirror* or *grandiose transference.* Together he called them the *selfobject transferences,* meaning that insofar as we gain what we need from another to maintain the cohesion of our self, the other is not at that moment an individual in his or her own right—in psychoanalytic language an *object*—but a source of supply for the self. In other words, Kohut understood, in keeping with all that has been learned about attachment (Karen 1994), that human beings are social animals, that initially our very lives and our development depend on the physical and psychological support of those around us, and that throughout life—especially in times of crisis—the meaningful participation of others is essential for the cohesion of the self. Kohut taught us that, contrary to common belief, maturity and independence should not be equated with some sort of freestanding isolation; quite the contrary, the freedom and ability to seek and obtain age-appropriate selfobject input when and if needed—the *mature selfobject experience,* as he called it—are essential aspects of adulthood and of psychological health.

I have found these contributions to be of great practical benefit in my clinical work, and in combination with my clinical experience I have distilled from them what I call the developmental model for psychotherapy. The latter will unfold as we work our way through the clinical illustrations that provide the opportunity to clarify its details, rationale, and application. The thrust of what is to follow is that through the use of the developmental model a readily mastered, highly effective, and widely applicable brief psychotherapy has become a reality.

DOING BRIEF PSYCHOTHERAPY

I

The Developmental Model

CHAPTER 1

Setting a Goal and Focusing the Treatment: Denise Taft

THE UTILITY of the developmental model lies in the help it gives us in finding and implementing the shortest effective treatment route for all patients. In this chapter and the next, I begin to introduce the components of the model with two cases presented to me for consultation in a residents' seminar. The first patient, Ms. Taft, would in all probability have been eliminated from consideration in the selection process used by short-term treatment clinics in academic settings, but discouraging and confusing as her situation may have seemed initially, that would have done her an injustice.

DENISE TAFT

A resident psychiatrist in his second year of training presented the case. The patient, Denise Taft, was fifty years old, divorced, and unemployed. When asked why she had come to the clinic, she said, "I am here on account of Jason." Jason was her former live-in boyfriend. A year prior to her appearance at the clinic, the patient had thrown

Jason out of her home, because he was abusive and alcoholic and refused to get a job. Initially, Ms. Taft was pleased to have freed herself and adamantly refused to consider Jason's repeated pleas for forgiveness. She felt fine as long as Jason continued to ask for reconciliation, but then, some months earlier, he had moved in with another woman and stopped calling her. Since then, the patient said she had been depressed. She experienced palpitations and spells of crying. She could not stop thinking about Jason, had thoughts of suicide (though she had made no attempts or plans in that direction), was disorganized, and could not seem to get anything done. For two months prior to coming to the clinic, she just did not seem to care about anything or anyone.

Denise's early history was fraught with loss and disappointment. She was raised by her mother, with whom, she said, she had a good relationship; her father left the family when she was two years old. Her mother told her that her father was alcoholic and abusive; eventually she divorced him. He would visit the family periodically, but the man to whom Denise became quite attached was her mother's second husband. Denise's stepfather clearly preferred her older sister to her, however, and she became very envious of that relationship. The patient was still not on good terms with her sister, her only sibling.

Denise did not have many friends as a child and had only an occasional date in high school. When she was seventeen, her first boyfriend impregnated her, and though she was not in love with him, they married shortly thereafter. She divorced him after fifteen years and two children. Her daughter, now living in another city, had dropped out of high school and become a prostitute. Her son had been a gang member and drug dealer, but he had managed to extricate himself from that life and was now married and had a steady job.

"Anything else?" I asked.

"No, that's basically what I know about her," said the resident therapist.

The students in the seminar and the therapist agreed on the probable recurrent dynamic patterns behind the patient's presenting complaint and her dysphoria: Ms. Taft was symbolically living out a traumatic pattern from childhood. Unconsciously attempting to right past injuries inflicted on her by her father's abandonment and her stepfather's lack of interest, she had succeeded only in replicating what had hurt her earlier. Her marriage was in many ways a carbon copy of her mother's failed union; in her interaction with Jason, she felt vindicated as long as it was she who abandoned him and she who asserted her lack of interest in resuming the relationship. When the tables were turned, however, she experienced the reversal as a repetition of the childhood trauma, and it precipitated depressive symptoms.

These speculations were to some extent corroborated by the course Ms. Taft's therapy had taken in the five sessions the therapist had had with her. When the therapist clarified for Ms. Taft the repetitive patterns he discerned in her relationships with men, she supported his interpretation by recalling and reexperiencing the emotional distress she would feel when her father, who seemed to care for her when he saw her on his visits, disappeared once more. Equally significant was the manner in which she treated her appointments with the therapist. She did not come for her second session as scheduled; instead, she called the clinic secretary a few hours later with an excuse for missing the appointment but made no attempt to reschedule it. When the therapist then called her to find out what she intended to do about treatment, she was clearly pleased by his interest and happy to arrange for the next meeting. This pattern repeated itself between the second and third and the fourth and fifth appointments. Her need to reassure herself in this way both that she was wanted and cared for and that now it was she who was leaving while "father" was pursuing was interpreted early on to the patient by the therapist. Ms. Taft seemed to understand this explanation, but awareness did not lead to improvement in her condition or change her behavior. The therapist, feeling at a loss as to how to proceed, had brought her case to the seminar as a problem. What, he wanted to know, should he do now?

At this point I think anyone in a clinic setting will recognize a familiar type of case history. And one might predict that Ms. Taft could very well become one of those patients who are passed from one graduating resident to a beginning one, ad infinitum, discussing with each in turn, week after week, the frustration of her failed and failing relationships. Each therapist provides an understanding ear but wonders why neither continued "empathic listening" nor the "insight" given to her into the connection between her childhood traumas and her present disappointments seems to make a significant difference in her outlook or her behavior, while the trial of one antidepressant medication after another fails to do more than let her vegetate a bit more comfortably.

The problem Ms. Taft's therapist and the seminar students have created for themselves is that so far the patient has been equated with her presenting problem. Put that way, the flaw in their thinking is self-evident; we do not treat problems, we treat people, and people add up to more than the sum of their respective problems. From that viewpoint we do not know much about Ms. Taft as yet.

No one is without strengths, and those strengths can more often than not offset an individual's deficits or conflicts. Although our work continually depends on it, we therapists do not emphasize enough what the biologist C. H. Waddington (1966) has called the self-righting tendency. There is a strong pull toward establishing or reestablishing order in living systems that opposes the entropic tendency of the universe.

When I meet new patients, I always make it a point to assess their strengths, listening for what went right in their lives as well as what seems to have gone wrong. It is the patients' strengths that will give me the leverage I need to help them to do something about their problems. The majority of people who come to us for help have what it takes to turn their situations around in relatively short order, given appropriate psychotherapeutic assistance. The problem is not that most patients do not have a great deal to contribute to their treatment but, rather, that therapists do not look for it. The notion that a patient's difficulty today expresses a fundamental flaw that needs to be corrected by going back to childhood and working from the ground up is probably the greatest obstacle in the way of learning how to do brief psychotherapy. I, as a psychoanalyst with an abiding interest in the psychological life of infants, would be the last to dispute the evidence that everything we think or do today has its roots in what has gone before, all the way back to day one. But that goes for our strengths as well as our weaknesses. I do my best not to forget that the person who consults me has so far managed to function and get something out of life without me and that the job of therapy is to further the patient's development rather than start from scratch to correct or revamp it.

When we work successfully, we are not solving patients' problems per se; rather we are helping them to use or enhance what they have on the plus side to minimize, offset, and occasionally eradicate what is on the minus side. We are helping them to right themselves so that *they* will be in a position to solve the problems that brought them to us in the first place. From the moment a patient calls me to set up an appointment, I listen for both problems and assets, strengths as well as weaknesses: "Doctor, I need to come to see you, but I can't do it this week; my mother has to go in for an operation, and I want to be with her till she's out of danger." Though I will have to wait to hear this patient's complaint, I have already heard something of the patient's strengths.

Once the patient's strengths have been provisionally established and we know something of what we have to work with, we can zero in on the difficulties the patient seems to be having, with a view to making a salutary difference. The developmental model enables us then to construct a decision tree that will let us address precisely what we believe needs to be worked with in that patient's situation. If we succeed in furthering the therapeutic process, we know why we did so and can take direction from that; if we do not, then at least we know which option failed and can systematically explore another.

Accordingly, I asked the presenting resident, "Now that I know something of what is 'wrong' with Ms. Taft—or, more correctly, what she believes to be her trouble—what is there that is 'right' about the patient?" Did Ms. Taft, I wanted to know, ever do anything that brought her and those around her some joy? Having so often been disappointed in her relationships with men, was there any kind of accomplishment in her life that might enhance her sense of worth and well-being?

When the resident first recounted Ms. Taft's situation as he understood it, his voice had sounded resigned and almost apologetic for presenting us with such a disastrous case. When I asked him to think about the patient's accomplishments and areas of competence, however, his voice became stronger, and he conveyed a sense of excitement. It was as if he were talking about a different person.

It turned out that Ms. Taft, in spite of her limited education, had early on become quite an accomplished player of reed instruments. She appeared with various small groups at weddings, parties, and an occasional club date and was able to support herself in that fashion. She continued to work after she was married and had children. Her husband, being mostly unemployed, was left to watch the children. When Ms. Taft found out that her husband had begun to abuse their daughter sexually, she confronted him, and he became violent. In the struggle that ensued, he fractured her jaw and broke many of her teeth. Shortly thereafter the couple was divorced. The patient found that because of the damage to her lower face, she could no longer function as a musician, even after reconstructive surgery. Instead, she became a waitress at one of the restaurants where she had previously performed. She liked this work, and apparently people liked her; her tips were excellent, and she ended up making more money than she had as an instrumentalist. She had worked in this job until two years prior to coming for therapy, when she had quit; she had not worked since.

I think we all shared the sense of admiration for Ms. Taft that her therapist's voice reflected as he told us how, because of her husband's brutalization, she had had to change careers and had not only survived but prevailed. It deserves to be emphasized that the therapist—who is talented, teachable, hardworking, and all other good things a resident psychiatrist should be—was perfectly aware of this side of Ms. Taft's life but simply had not considered it to be pertinent information, because it was not part of the problem; that it could well be part of the solution was not yet within his theoretical frame of reference.

The frame of reference I have in mind is what I call the *developmental model* of psychotherapy. To help me to get a rough idea of what I as a therapist have to work with when I evaluate a patient's situation, I subdivide development into five sectors: affect and reason, attachment, psychosexuality, autonomy, and creativity (see figure 1.1). The category labeled *other* indicates that this organizing template or guide, like each of the other components of the developmental model, is open to additions and corrections whenever they are indicated as a result of clinical experience or germane discoveries in other fields.

I should add a word about the sector of development labeled *affect/reason*. Previously I bowed to custom and called it *affect/cognition* (Basch 1988). But not only is that wrong, it misleads our therapeutic efforts by mistakenly relegating affect to something apart from thought. Affect and reason go hand in hand; they are inseparable in real life and represent respectively the contributions of the limbic system and the neocortex to the process we call thought or cognition. *Cognition (cognoscere)* simply means coming to know, and we come to know or cognize through affective experiences as much as, if not more

Figure 1.1: Sectors of Development

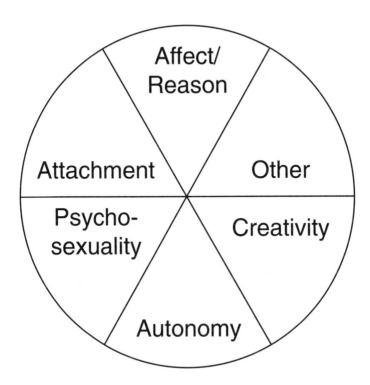

Reprinted by permission from Michael Franz Basch, *Practicing Psychotherapy: A Casebook* (New York: Basic Books, 1992), p. 23.

than, through reasoning (Basch 1988). The artificial separation we must make between the two is only for didactic purposes; we can talk about only one thing at a time. By the same token, the division of psychotherapies into cognitive and affective or dynamic is equally misleading. Developmental psychotherapy approaches the patient through whatever route promises to be most effective, whether that is affect, reason, or, for that matter, behavior. In real time they all come together anyway. It is this flexibility that permits treatment that would otherwise be lengthy and often less successful to become brief and meaningful.

Now that we had a better idea of Ms. Taft's functioning overall, the case looked very different. Although there was trouble in the attachment sector of development, autonomy was highly developed, and there was no evidence that the sectors of affect/reason or creativity were significantly lacking. There was a great deal to work with here, but I needed some more information. Why, I wanted to know, did she stop working two years ago in a job that she enjoyed, thereby losing the self-integrating function that comes with success in one's occupation? The answer to that the therapist could not tell us. Without it I felt I could not render an opinion on the patient's case or recommend an approach to treatment.

The importance of this issue lies in the fact that it addresses another aspect of development that is crucial for evaluating a patient's past and present functioning. In a previous publication (Basch 1988) I have discussed the validity and advantage of the so-called competence model of mental functioning. It is summarized in what I call the *developmental spiral* (see figure 1.2). Striving for competence—that is, promoting a situation in which one is reasonably well adapted to the environment while at the same time meeting one's own needs—is universal and fundamental to all behavior, without exception.

Figure 1.2: The Developmental Spiral

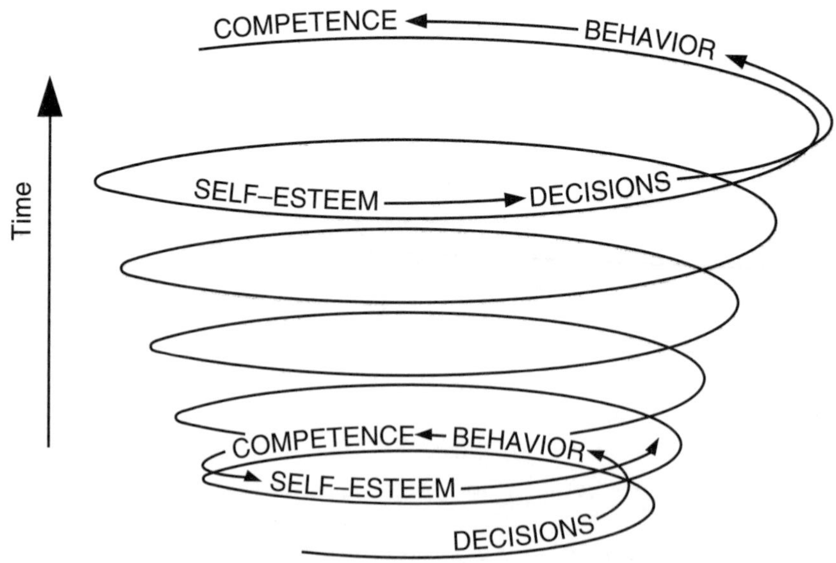

Reprinted by permission from Michael Franz Basch, *Understanding Psychotherapy* (New York: Basic Books, 1988), p. 29.

Optimally there is a steady progression beginning with making a decision, then implementing it behaviorally, finding oneself competent, and thereby increasing one's self-esteem—pleasure in one's functioning. The spiral of development serves as a guide for both our evaluation of a particular patient's situation and our choice of intervention. In assessing what is wrong with a patient, we are identifying the area of incompetence that has led to a diminished self-worth; then comes the question of how we will use the patient's strengths to get or keep the developmental spiral moving in the right direction. We have to decide where on the developmental spiral as it pertains to that particular learning process we can most appropriately intervene, to help the person function once more as a center of initiative (Kohut 1971).

I explained to my students that we were at an intersection in the road with Ms. Taft, and that the answer to the question as to why she left the workforce would determine in which direction we should travel with her to reestablish a sense of competence and restore the cohesive self. We had to reassess her strengths. When I ask to hear what is "right" with a patient, I am addressing the issue of what there is to work with. Ms. Taft's complaint made it clear that she was functioning incompetently in the sector of attachment; she was finding her sense of well-being tied to the behavior of her former boyfriend. But we saw that she had been able to accomplish a great deal that was satisfying to her in the sector of autonomy, in fashioning a career. The solidity of her capacity in that sector was shown by her resilience in recovering from the loss of her livelihood and making an entry into a different line of work. Did something occur in the area of autonomy that rendered her incompetent here as well, that so undermined her self-esteem that, as we tried to figure out where and how to intervene, we could not count on that sector of development for therapeutic leverage? Or was there an extraneous reason for her withdrawal that left her sense of self-worth with respect to autonomy intact? I needed to know why she had given up functioning in the world of work and relinquished the self-esteem that that gave her, so that I could determine what it might take to bring the self-righting tendency into play.

I did not have long to wait for my answer; the matter resolved itself even faster than I imagined it might. The therapist had clearly understood what I had said and used it creatively. When our seminar met a month later, he reported on the subsequent session with the patient.

Ms. Taft once again brought up her complaints regarding her erstwhile boyfriend. This time the therapist explained to her our striving for a sense of self-worth and related it to her need to be pursued. Withdrawing from Jason and then being pursued again by him had served that purpose. Of course, he went on to say, when Jason broke the cycle by moving in with another woman, her self-esteem was understandably shattered. The patient corroborated this hypothesis by spontaneously recalling a number of incidents in which a nagging dysphoria had been instantaneously alleviated when she was singled out for commendation or preferred to others.

The therapist then talked to her about other ways of getting self-esteem and mentioned how much happier she had seemed to be when she was working. Why did she quit waitressing two years ago he wanted to know. Ms. Taft explained that at that time her son's girlfriend gave birth to his baby, and Ms. Taft agreed to stay home and take care of the infant until the two were married and established their own household. That happened after a year, and she just never went back to work. "Do you think it might be worthwhile trying to do that now?" the therapist asked. Ms. Taft did not respond, and he was not sure he had been heard. When she missed the next appointment, he once again called her. She said that since her last session she had gotten a job with her former employer, who was delighted to have her back. She was working as a waitress, felt good, and did not think she needed further treatment. She had been meaning to get in touch with him, she said, but had been so busy that she kept putting it off.

This last session the therapist had with the patient highlighted significant strengths in Ms. Taft that could be turned to good advantage in therapy. Indeed, even in the area of attachment, she showed strength in her willingness to take over the care of her grandchild while the parents were getting settled. (This is a nice illustration of how as we work with a patient we constantly update and refine the organization made possible by the various components of the model of development.)

In terms of the developmental spiral the therapist was dealing with the patient on the level of decision making, pointing out an alternative that she might choose to think about. Ms. Taft then independently completed the developmental spiral, implementing the decision with appropriate behavior and regaining competence by functioning as a self-actuating individual, a center of initiative. Her sense of self-worth was restored not only by returning to the working world that she knew well but also by the validation of being welcomed back by her boss as a desirable member of the team. She could then do for herself what needed to be done to maintain that cohesive state.

We should note that as far as the therapist could tell from the patient's report and tone of voice on the telephone, her depressive symptomatology was no longer in evidence. Depression and other forms of psychopathology are indicators that people are trying but failing to cope adequately with some developmental challenge (Basch 1988). Symptoms are alleviated as patients once again take charge of their lives, as Ms. Taft did. This, by the way, is equally true for psychopharmacologic therapy. It is a mistake to say that those depressions that respond to medication have been cured by the drug. Psychotropic drugs do not cure patients any more than we psychotherapists do. When successful, psychotherapy and drugs, alone or in combination, remove the barriers to a person's competent functioning, and therein lies the cure.

After the case and its outcome were presented, the students in the seminar raised a number of questions. Some felt that perhaps Ms. Taft should have been encouraged to return for therapy. She might have taken as a rejection the therapist's comment that she felt better when she was working. Could the reason that she did not come back have been that she thought he was saying, "Pull yourself together; don't depend on me to do the job for you"? I thought, however, that had she felt hurt, she would not have sounded so chipper and pleased with herself. Most likely she would have reverted to form and asked to make another appointment once the therapist had "kissed and made up" by "pursuing" her once again with a follow-up phone call. Instead, as the developmental spiral would predict, when she found a way to function competently and restore her sense of worth, she quite correctly concluded that she no longer needed treatment. She may not have parted in the most polite fashion, but that was beside the point.

The students also expressed concern that the problem of Ms. Taft's relationships with men had not been resolved. My response was, Don't underestimate the momentum generated when you help patients to remove obstacles to growth. Ms. Taft was now a different person from the patient who came into therapy. There was justifiable hope that, with her self-esteem once again in good order, the illusory sense of competence she obtained from gaining the interest of unreliable men would no longer be needed. If, however, she found herself falling into the same trap, she could always return for further treatment. What had been done in brief therapy to restore her to competent functioning in areas where she was free to do so would stand her in good stead if that did happen.

The students continued to marvel at Ms. Taft's rapid response to the therapist's intervention. What would have happened, they wondered, if it had not worked? I pointed out that Ms. Taft responded so quickly because her therapist looked beyond her immediate complaint to the basic issue responsible for her dysphoria—namely, that she was not functioning as a center of initiative—and showed her that it was within her power to do something about that. Orienting the patient by reframing the problem is often enough to turn the tide. Of course, if a therapist assumes, as is so often done, that good treatment always begins at the beginning rather than with what is already in place, then there are no Ms. Tafts.

In essence there are five ways in which anyone solves problems and restores order, and these give us as therapists the options we have potentially available, alone or in combination, to help our patients restore competent functioning and with it their sense of self-esteem: (1) orienting the patient by reframing the problem in developmental terms; (2) assisting the patient in gaining the necessary skills to deal with the problem; (3) correcting deficits or conflicts that are keeping the patient from reaching out affectively to others for emotional support and understanding; (4) removing obstacles to reflection so as to let the patient think clearly about problems; and (5) helping the patient to develop the capacity for narrative, the ability to communicate effectively to those whose understanding and advice they seek. Together these options make up what I call a guide to problem-solving intervention (see figure 1.3).*

Since I wanted Ms. Taft's therapist to reframe her problem and help her see that it was in her interest to look to her strengths in autonomy

---

*The "Guide to Problem-Solving Intervention" is a modification and extension of "The Search for Competence" (Basch 1992), figure 3.2, p. 37.

Figure 1.3: A Guide to Problem-Solving Intervention

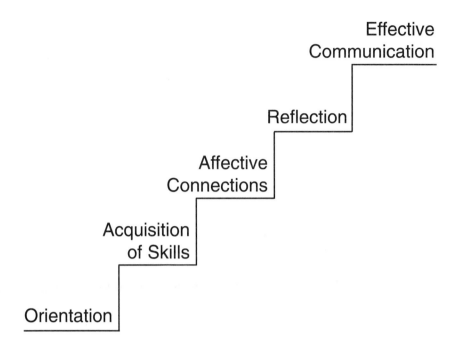

rather than to focus on attachment, where she was weak, it made sense to me to have him orient her to this concept and see what happened. But if it had not worked, or if circumstances had been different, then there would have been no problem with intervening on another level. If, for example, Ms. Taft had told her therapist that she had stopped work because she felt she was being treated unfairly and her boss would not listen to her, then I would have suggested that he discuss with her how she presented her complaints and why they fell on deaf ears—that is, explore her narrative capacities. If she had said that she had stopped work because the job was becoming too difficult, then I would have recommended that the therapist learn from Ms. Taft the ins and outs of her position and, if she really lacked the skills to perform as she ought, investigate what she might do to become proficient or what alternative work might be within her abilities. Throughout, the emphasis would be on her coming to grips with the need to function by drawing on her strengths and in that way restoring her sense of self-worth.

THE DIFFERENCE BETWEEN BRIEF PSYCHOTHERAPY AND PSYCHOANALYSIS

In the goal of therapy, there is basically no difference between brief psychotherapy and psychoanalysis, but in the technique used to get that result, there is a great deal of difference. When we psychoanalysts tell patients that they are in for the long haul, we are making the assumption that whatever their psychological strengths may be, as revealed by their past history, it is our best judgment, given the nature of their difficulties, that what they have achieved psychologically is not enough to turn the tide. Therefore, we must ask them to take the time and make the effort to work with us to retrace their development, find the fault lines in it, and together repair the damage. In our professional opinion, only then will they have what is needed to take control of their lives with the reasonable hope that they will be able to make the most of their abilities and opportunities. That does not mean, however, that it is a foregone conclusion that the preferred road to recovery for every patient is always the roundabout one; quite the contrary. I learned nothing from the presentation of Ms. Taft's complaint and history that persuaded me that an answer to her present difficulty necessitated an investigation and dissection of the hidden aspects of her childhood.

When I am doing a psychoanalysis, because in my best judgment there is no other way to get at that particular person's problem, I use a highly specialized technique to try to reconstruct with the patient what "competence" and "self-esteem" may have meant to them at different times in their life, what decisions they made and what behavior they implemented to reach their goals, and why they failed to achieve the desired result. But all this is done in the interest of freeing the patient to do whatever they are now able to do about the problem that brought them for analysis in the first place, so that who they are—that is what they aim for and how they try to get there—has been altered in some significant way by the analytic experience. Although the time element is dramatically altered in psychoanalysis, in other respects this is not so different from what we hope to accomplish in brief or any other psychotherapy.

When the proactive, incisive stance I advocate and have begun to outline does not prove effective, its failure may indicate that time will be required to work through the patient's unconscious defenses in the transference to the therapist. That is the work that our training in psychoanalysis and dynamic psychotherapy has prepared us to do. I do not think we will fail to identify those patients who need either prolonged supportive therapy, or who require an opportunity to recapitulate and repair the defects in their psychological development, or whose resistances are such that only an analytic approach can hope to be effective. I will discuss these situations in greater detail in chapter 7. Our problem as a group has been that we have equated dynamic with *regressive* therapy and have not learned that positive developmental changes can be brought about in many, probably most, patients with a *progressive* technique. It is best to think of every patient as a potential short-term patient. One will not damage a patient or preclude open-ended therapy or psychoanalysis if the attempt to do brief therapy reveals that the patient requires a different approach.

So far I have introduced three aspects of the developmental model: the sectors of development (figure 1.1), the developmental spiral (figure 1.2), and the guide to problem-solving intervention (figure 1.3). These and the other components of the model to follow permit the therapist to transform the patient's phenomenological description into a developmental diagnosis. I think it is already clear how this moves us beyond the commonly used diagnostic criteria based on symptom clusters, which do not tell us what to do for the patient to whom a particular nosologic label is attached. The developmental model identifies the location and nature of the specific incompetencies behind the issues that trouble the patient and, in doing so, clarifies the options open to the therapist. A decision tree is created, an if-so-then-so progression that guides the therapist's activity.

CHAPTER 2

Restoring Competence: Ralph Jerome

IT IS IMPORTANT to identify the affect operating in a patient at any given time, for in the final analysis it is the affect attached to a particular decision that initiates behavior and determines the intensity with which it is pursued. Let us see, therefore, how affect is integrated into the developmental model.

Following the work of Silvan Tomkins as explicated by Nathanson (1994a), I have organized the basic affect ranges into three groups (figure 2.1). (Boredom and sadness, which I had previously considered to be affects in their own right, are better understood as forms of distress [Nathanson 1994b].) These basic affects begin to operate at or shortly after birth, and although the language of emotions becomes increasingly complex as we mature, we can always get our psychotherapeutic bearings by identifying where the patient is operating on this scale. Ms. Taft's therapy can serve as an example.

In Ms. Taft's case, as with all patients who have depressions, distress was prominent. When her therapist reminded her of the self-esteem and attendant pleasure she had derived from her work at the restaurant, she apparently experienced, either then or after the session, an awakening of interest—a transition from negative to positive

Figure 2.1: Ranges of Basic Affect

Positive Affects
Interest—Excitement
Enjoyment—Joy
Neutral Affects
Surprise—Startle
Negative Affects
Distress—Anguish
Anger—Rage
Fear—Terror
Shame—Humiliation
Contempt
Disgust

Adapted from D. L. Nathanson, ed., "Shame, Compassion, and the 'Border-line Personality,'" *Psychiatric Clinics of North America 17* (1994), 791.

affect—sufficient to lead her to apply for her former job. That her therapy could safely be discontinued was signaled by the obvious joy in her tone of voice when she told the therapist how she felt in her new situation. Her affect let us know that the developmental spiral was once again moving in the right direction.

In the following case, an understanding of the developmental significance of the patient's intense negative affect permitted brief psychotherapy to deal successfully with a crisis that could well have had serious consequences for both the patient and his family.

RALPH JEROME

The case of Ralph Jerome, like that of Ms. Taft, was presented in a residents' seminar. It provides a further illustration of the axiom that if there is to be any psychotherapy other than long-term therapy, therapists must learn to begin working on those issues that are interfering with a patient's functioning in the here and now; only if that fails to restore the patient to competence should the therapist engage in lengthier exploration.

The patient, Mr. Jerome, was a thirty-eight-year-old man who had been hospitalized to undergo a workup for severe hypertension and a possible stroke. Although he was found not to have suffered a cerebrovascular accident and his blood pressure was brought under good medical control, he became increasingly anxious, expressing the superstitious conviction that he was sure to die within the year, and psychiatric consultation was sought. Once it was established that the patient was not suicidal, he was discharged with appropriate medication for his blood pressure, to be followed in a psychiatric outpatient clinic for anxiety and depression.

As far as the patient knew, he had never been significantly anxious or depressed prior to the incident that hospitalized him. He had been working as a security guard when he noted that he had a bad headache and was dizzy. He ignored these symptoms and kept working, but several hours later he collapsed and was taken to the nearest emergency room; his hospitalization followed.

The patient told the resident psychiatrist that he was convinced that he would die because his father also had had high blood pressure and had died of a stroke at the age of thirty-nine, the very age that he, the patient, was now approaching. He was nineteen when his father died, he himself had a married son who was now nineteen years old, and his daughter-in-law had recently given birth to a son.

The replication of the chronological pattern convinced Mr. Jerome that fate had decreed his imminent demise. Although he was now living at home and had been told that he could resume his normal lifestyle as long as he took his medicine and came for periodic checkups, he had not gone back to work for fear that any exertion or excitement would bring about the dreaded stroke that would kill him. He was very nervous at home around the children of his second marriage (two daughters, aged twelve and eight), afraid that their noisy play or their occasional quarrels would be too upsetting for him and precipitate the fatal event. In other words, he was becoming a severely hypochondriacal invalid.

The resident described the patient's background and past history. Mr. Jerome was the only child of a divorced couple. His mother had deserted the family when he was twelve years old. She was an alcoholic and ran off to live in a common-law relationship with her husband's brother. When Ralph was sixteen years old, his father remarried. Ralph "hated" his stepmother, who apparently vented her frequent rages, whatever their source might be, on him. When he was nineteen years old, his father, as I have mentioned, died of a stroke induced by severe hypertension. The father, however, had also been a diabetic and an alcoholic who ignored his illness, continued to drink to excess, and never followed medical advice. Both the internist and the consulting psychiatrist had taken great pains to point out to the patient that his situation was very different from that of his father. Mr. Jerome was neither alcoholic nor diabetic, and his blood pressure was under excellent control. He was repeatedly told that there was every reason to believe that he would live out a normal life span, but he would not be reassured. The anxiolytic and antidepressant medications prescribed for him seemed to have little or no effect on his psychological symptoms.

I asked if anything else was known of the patient's background. We then learned that after his father's death, Mr. Jerome decided that he could not live with his hated stepmother and would make a life for himself. His girlfriend was five months pregnant when his father died, and they decided to get married. Having previously dropped out of school, he reenrolled to qualify for a high school diploma. During that time, he supported himself and his new wife with part-time jobs. After he graduated, he went to work as a warehouse helper and attended a tuition-free junior college at night.

Finding that the job in the warehouse was leading nowhere, Mr. Jerome answered an ad for security guards and switched occupations. He worked the night shift, and that permitted him to transfer to a four-year college and continue studying in the daytime for a bachelor's degree. (Although he now had a degree in accounting, he never had the confidence in his skills to work in that field on a full-time basis. He did some freelance work at income tax time and occasional bookkeeping for acquaintances.) He enjoyed the job with the security guard company, which had good fringe benefits, and over the years he worked his way up to the rank of lieutenant in charge of the night shift at several office buildings.

Mr. Jerome's first marriage did not turn out well. He obtained a divorce after his wife, repeating his mother's pattern, ran away with one of his distant cousins. He remarried some years later, as his father had done; until then he raised his son alone. The patient's second marriage seemed to be solid and satisfying for both himself and his spouse—that is, it was satisfying and rewarding until his constant nervous preoccupation with sickness and death began to create an uncomfortably tense situation in the home. His wife and his two daughters were now becoming increasingly anxious with the pressure the patient's condition imposed on them.

I asked the residents in the seminar to discuss their understanding of the case and plan its management. They were fairly unanimous in their evaluation and recommendations. All were impressed by the patient's fatalistic belief in predestination; they speculated that Mr. Jerome, compelled to reenact the past, might unconsciously have contributed to his first wife's having essentially repeated the pattern of his mother's desertion of his father. The residents felt that we were in no position to give the patient the reassurance that he sought. Like any of us, he indeed might die unexpectedly, so no one—least of all a physician—could in good conscience give him an unqualified promise that what he feared would not happen. The students' recommendation was that the therapist continue to explore the history of the patient's relationship to his father, mother, and stepmother. "Why?" I wanted to know. Their answer was that his anxiety, though precipitated by his physical problems, was probably related to deeper psychological causes that opportunistically attached themselves to his somatic difficulties. Fainting, falling down, learning that strange and dangerous processes within his body and out of his awareness were threatening his very existence are the sorts of happenings that lend themselves readily to the representation of deeper issues. More specifically, several students felt that there was a likelihood that Mr. Jerome's fear of death might represent an unresolved oedipal problem, that it was an indicator of the patient's ambivalence toward his deceased father. As with Ms. Taft's case, the students, guided by the concept that "dynamic" implies "regressive," opted for an open-ended exploration of Mr. Jerome's life in the belief that his cure depended on explaining and linking his present symptoms to the traumas of his childhood.

Although I could not at this point rule out the need for such an approach, I was not so quick to adopt it just yet. There are two ways to listen to Mr. Jerome's history. If one sees patients as victims who need us to build psychic structure from the ground up, then one hears, as my residents did, a sad story of a boy bereft of his mother, not by death but by desertion. Desertion is worse than death; from the child's viewpoint, she had a choice to make between her son and her lover, and whatever feelings she had for Ralph were not enough to hold her. His father did take over, but one wonders how his alcoholism affected his parental functioning. Then, when a maternal figure came on the scene in the form of a stepmother, she apparently made things worse rather than better for Ralph. He was married before he was really mature enough, only to be deserted once more. As had happened with his mother and stepmother, he was rejected for the third time by a woman in whom he placed or wanted to place trust. He beat the odds, not only graduating from high school but working his way through college, and got a degree in accounting, but then he was unable to make use of his education professionally. Learning that he had hypertension and had almost had a stroke was the last straw in an unremitting series of psychological injuries. Helpless and hopeless, he came to us so that we might share with him our understanding of what he had suffered. We would help him by giving him the opportunity to make conscious his pain and disappointment, to relive the past in the therapeutic situation, and thereby begin to build a stronger ego, a healthier sense of self.

Using the developmental model to assess the patient, however, puts a significantly different light on the situation. Here was a man who had had an unfortunate childhood, an unsuccessful first marriage, and perhaps a professional disappointment. Nevertheless, Mr. Jerome seemed to have made a reasonable success of his life in that he was well adapted to the society in which he lived while getting what he needed from it; that is, he was happy with his family, enjoyed his occupation, and seemed to have the respect of those for and with whom he worked. That he had not only survived a trying childhood but accomplished all that he had was a testament to his psychological strength and, by implication, an indicator that we had a great deal to work with in assisting him in his recovery. As far as I was concerned, there was as yet no evidence that, if I were his therapist, I would need to connect the past to the present in order to mobilize his demonstrated psychological strengths.

In terms of the developmental model, Mr. Jerome seemed to have functioned well in the sectors of autonomy and attachment. His problem-solving ability was excellent, and his narrative as he told his story was still cohesive and coherent. Even his quasi-delusional explanation for his overwhelming anxiety hung together. On the spiral of development, the contrast between present and past was of course dramatic; at one time highly competent in the face of significant obstacles, he was now helpless. What was preventing him from using his considerable resources to cope with his present situation? The answer lies in the fact that affectively he was trapped at the upper end of the fear/terror range. In and of itself, fear can be salutary in that it mobilizes a person's resources to cope with perceived danger. When fear becomes a disorganizing rather than an organizing force, however, it destroys the ability to make meaningful decisions. As would be expected, behavior suffers, incompetence undermines self-confidence, and we encounter a developmental spiral in reverse. Eventually patients find themselves helpless and unable to recover their psychological balance. I thought of Mr. Jerome's superstitious conviction that he was fated to die at the age his father did as a rationalization, a last-ditch, self-righting attempt that, painful as it was, still formed a core around which his self-concept could be organized. It was clear to me that his delusion—his protection against total disorganization, anomie, and the disintegration of what Heinz Kohut (1971) calls the cohesive self—would not be relinquished until his fear abated.

My sense of Mr. Jerome's situation was that if I were his therapist, I certainly would not tuck my psychoanalytic experience under the couch and forget about it, but I also would not consider psychoanalysis or any other open-ended regressive approach to be what he needed or could use at this point in his illness. Even if my students' guesswork were on the mark and his near-stroke had had such an effect because, on the unconscious level, it represented a punishment for an oedipal transgression, would exploration of this possibility be therapeutically feasible? No, quite the contrary: Any attempt at psychoanalytically oriented therapy, which relies on patients' ability to relinquish conscious control over their thought processes while simultaneously reflecting on the results of that experience, would only intensify Mr. Jerome's panic.

Developmentally speaking, there are two ways to manage fear, which can be used alone or in combination. One can cope by drawing on the sector of autonomy, using past experience or developing new skills to manage whatever is threatening, or one can turn to the sector of attachment and reach out to others for help. Mr. Jerome was evidently unable to do either; indeed, that inability accounted for his panic. Knowing from the patient's past history that in all probability he had the requisite psychological strengths to adapt to his physical illness, it was now up to the therapist to determine the technique that would permit engagement of the patient and the mobilization of his strengths.

We already knew from the attempts of his physicians to reason with Mr. Jerome that intervention on the level of reflection (see figure 1.3) had not proved possible. He was fixated on his obsessive numerologic concern with death. The fear was so strong that even the sympathy of his family and his physicians was not helping him regain his balance.

When anxiety mounts to the point that people can neither trust themselves nor others, optimally two things should happen. First, legitimate authority should reassert itself: "Damn the torpedoes, full speed ahead," "There is nothing to fear but fear itself," "Daddy is here and you are safe." Second, the one who has panicked should be shown that under that protective umbrella it is possible to learn to gain or regain control and next time be better prepared to handle that and other stressful situations. I described to my students in our seminar how I pictured a session with Mr. Jerome:

PATIENT: Everybody says I don't have anything to worry about, but I know I do.

THERAPIST: You bet you've got something to worry about. High blood pressure—or hypertension, as we physicians call it—is not something to be taken lightly, and so I am glad you are taking your medication and watching your diet. I called your internist this morning, and he told me you checked out very well last week. That's great. Have you started that exercise program they told you about?

PATIENT: I'm scared, Doc. What if it's too much for me?

THERAPIST: It won't be; you won't be asked to do anything that is too much for you. (*Notice that here Mr. Jerome is voicing a not unreasonable concern, to which I give a reassuring answer.*)

PATIENT: I just know I'm going to die like my father did. I'll never live to see forty. (*He reverts, as would be expected, to his pathologic preoccupation. The fact that for a moment he could deal realistically with his illness is an encouraging sign, however, and leads me to persist in the tack I have taken.*)

THERAPIST: I know you *believe* you will die within the year, but you won't.

PATIENT: How do you know?

THERAPIST: We have great medicine for what ails you, and you're a good patient who follows instructions. You will not die.

PATIENT: I know I will.

THERAPIST: What you *don't* know is how your system works. *I* know you *won't* die because I'm a doctor, and we learn all that in medical school. All *you* know is that bad stuff is happening inside of you that you have no control over, and that scares the pants off of you. I can appreciate that. But I'm going to let you in on what I know, so you'll know too what's happening, and why you will not die.

> (*Here a student interrupted: "What if he does die before he is forty?" My answer was, "Who is to bear witness? If Mr. Jerome has the unlikely misfortune to see his prophecy fulfilled, it is of course possible that sometime in the—I hope distant—future, when and if we meet in another locale, I will be called to account for my mistaken prognosis."*)

PATIENT: But I . . .

THERAPIST: (*Seemingly not hearing the patient, taking out pencil and paper and drawing a diagram*) Here, see, this is your heart. It's just a big pump. Its job is to push your blood through these pipes— we call them arteries—and, in your case, they were building up this cholesterol crap on their walls. So the pipes were getting stiffer and narrower, and the heart had to push harder and harder to get the right amount of blood through to the rest of the body. So the blood was going through at higher and higher pressure— that's your high blood pressure—and the worry is that the pressure will get too high for a pipe and it will burst.

PATIENT: Like when the plumbing freezes in the winter. (*This is the turning point; fear has changed to interest. The patient is reorienting himself to the reality of his situation by picking up on my analogy and carrying it further. Once positive affect is mobilized, his coping skills and creativity can once again come into play.*)

THERAPIST: Exactly. When a pipe bursts we call it a stroke. Fortunately, you had warning signs that your pipes were under strain before that happened. The medicine that you are taking now relaxes the arteries—the pipes—so the heart doesn't have to work so hard to get the juice through. So, here, let's draw the arteries a lot wider; there goes the high blood pressure back to normal. At the same time, the diet that you are following not only prevents cholesterol buildup, it works like Lime-Away and dissolves the deposits that are already there. So I'll do some erasing here. The exercise program that you will be starting helps with that, also, and tones up all your muscles as well. When your muscles are toned up, they get the blood circulating more efficiently, and that saves the heart even more work. So now you are the boss of your body once more, and nothing bad will happen. As a matter of fact, you will probably live longer than people who haven't had the kind of scare you had and so don't live healthy—don't watch their diet, don't exercise, but smoke, and drink too much.

PATIENT: But how do I know that everything is okay again? I'm only going for checkups every six weeks now. Maybe he won't get the whole picture. (*In another sign of improvement, anxiety is attached to reasonable rather than delusional concerns. The patient is firmly oriented, showing that his delusional preoccupation was not evidence of a heretofore unsuspected psychotic process. He is now asking the doctor to work with him to develop coping skills that will permit him to function effectively.*)

THERAPIST: Excellent point. I want you to get hold of a blood pressure cuff that you can operate yourself and keep a daily record of what's happening in there. Measure it in the morning when you get up and at bedtime, but I also want you to take it—at least for a while—before and after you exercise, after sexual intercourse, and when you think something is getting to you—the kids, or the world generally. I know you are afraid that exertion, excitement, and upset are going to play hell with your pressure; let's see what actually happens.

PATIENT: But what if it goes up too high and I don't have an appointment with my doctor—my other doctor—for a couple of weeks?

THERAPIST: I want you to check in with me by phone and let me know what's happening. I'm going to give you a number and a time to call in the afternoon. Once we have a few days under our belt, we'll know what's needed, and I will help you make whatever arrangements are necessary with your internist. (*Although the patient is anxious, his fears are reasonable, and his anxiety can now be dealt with in a straightforward, supportive manner. Trusting the therapist, the patient no longer has to concoct fantastic explanations for his anxiety.*)

I told the seminar that if Mr. Jerome's therapist could accept my suggestions, incorporating them into his style of working, I would expect the patient's anxiety to give way rapidly to a sense of mastery over his illness. I would look for Mr. Jerome to be back at work within a few weeks and telling the therapist after five or six visits that he did not think he needed to come in anymore. At that point I would probably recommend that the therapist agree but suggest a follow-up visit in two weeks, then in a month, and then when and if needed. The follow-up visits would be used to reemphasize the patient's success in regaining control, and praise him for his efforts on his own behalf. Of course, as in any psychotherapy, if new issues of concern to the patient were to surface during the follow-up visits, these would be explored, and if further therapy were indicated appropriate recommendations would be made.

When our seminar next met, the therapist reported that he had tried my approach and that the patient seemed engaged by it. When the matter of taking his own blood pressure came up, Mr. Jerome eagerly interrupted and said that he knew of a place where one could rent one of those machines. After two more visits, the fear of death was not even mentioned, and the patient started to talk about going back to work. First, however, he wanted to take a vacation with his wife; her parents had offered to take care of the children. When he saw the therapist three weeks later, he said that he had decided not to go back to the job that was waiting for him with the security firm but instead, having talked at some length with his wife, he was going to take a chance and expand his accounting business. It turned out that once he had stopped being afraid of dying, he had begun investigating this possibility and had been encouraged by the response he got from potential clients. He told the therapist that the scare he had had made him realize that he ought to think about what he really wanted to do and do it now, rather than assuming that life was forever and he could get around to it tomorrow. The therapist validated the patient's resolution, and at the patient's request therapy was terminated.

This outcome provided a very nice demonstration of a patient's rapid climb on the problem-solving staircase (see figure 1.3). Once oriented and helped to acquire the skills he needed to handle the anxiety about his physical condition, he reflected on the broader implications of his experience and then submitted his conclusions to both his wife and the therapist for feedback.

My suggestions regarding Mr. Jerome's therapy relied in part on my understanding of the role that affect plays in a person's ongoing development, but another parameter of the developmental model determined the manner that I suggested for approaching and then overcoming the patient's paralyzing fear. In Ms. Taft's case we saw that the therapist's counsel mobilized her to make the most of her assets, restoring autonomy and competence. This meant that she was able to rely on the therapist as an auxiliary source of psychological strength. This is an aspect of attachment that usually operates silently, calling attention to itself only when it is absent. In psychoanalysis and dynamic psychotherapy it is subsumed under such terms as the *non-erotic positive transference* (Freud 1912a, 1912b), *basic trust* (Erikson 1950), *working alliance* or *therapeutic alliance* (Greenson 1967), and *self-object transference* (Basch 1991, 1994; Kohut 1977, 1984). The positive transference is, as Freud pointed out, the therapist's ally. The capacity to rely on the therapist's guidance and the support that the therapeutic process per se offers are essential for any and all psychotherapeutic work. The presence of the positive transference indicates that the therapist is being equated unconsciously with the loving and helpful parent the patient had or longed for, and once this transference has been made, the therapist's words carry all the authority, influence, and power of such a parent. Under the influence of the positive transference, a patient's sense of isolation, loneliness, and helplessness is sufficiently ameliorated to lower anxiety and permit the appropriate interventions of the therapist to have an effect. By the same token, until a meaningful connection can be made between patient and therapist, the latter's interventions—no matter how correct in principle—will fail to be effective.

Since without a positive transference the therapist's interventions are not useful to a patient, it is essential to use the patient's way of relating to the therapist to identify any problems in this area. Indeed, whether or not brief therapy is possible often depends on whether or not a positive transference is in place or can be quickly mobilized. If it turns out that before a positive transference can be formed the therapist has to help the patient work out a significant developmental deficit having its roots in infancy or early childhood, then long-term, open-ended work is often indicated. (As the case of Mr. Dale in chapter 4 will show, however, "often" does not mean "always.")

Heinz Kohut unbundled the positive transference and subdivided it into three components, which he termed the *twinship* or *alter ego transference*, the *idealizing transference*, and the *mirror transference* (Basch 1986; Kohut 1984). Combining what is known of attachment in infancy and childhood through direct observation (Karen 1994) and experiment (Meltzoff 1985, 1990; Stern 1985) with what Kohut contributed to our knowledge of attachment deficits in adult patients, we can identify three basic, interdependent human needs embodied by the positive transference: an underlying assumption that one will be sufficiently welcome and valued to make a meaningful bond possible, which I call the capacity for *kinship;* the freedom to feel protected by and utilize another's guidance, which I call the capacity for *reliance;* and the readiness to feel soothed, enriched, or encouraged by another's understanding, which I call the capacity for *validation*. Infant research (Meltzoff 1985, 1990), as well as clinical experience, shows that kinship, reliance, and validation form a developmental hierarchy (see figure 2.2) that has implications for technique (Basch 1992).

Nothing that could be called therapeutic will happen if there is no sense of kinship—that is, if the patient cannot sufficiently connect with the therapist to take for granted that there is a possibility of being understood, that whatever their individual differences may be they stand on common ground. If kinship is not in evidence, then the therapist must work on that issue first, to see whether a workable bond can be formed. (Several cases that illustrate this problem and the techniques that can be used to deal with it are discussed in the last part of this book.) Kinship provides the soil in which reliance can grow, but it does not ensure that growth, and when reliance does not

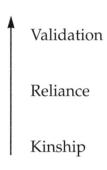

Figure 2.2: The Positive Transference

develop the therapist must work to make reliance possible. Once the patient can rely on the therapist, then the therapist's appropriate validation of the patient's efforts and achievements furthers progress within the developmental spiral.

In Ms. Taft's case the therapist's narrative made it clear to me that the requisite positive transference was in place. She showed no sort of mistrust that would have led me to doubt her capacity for bonding. She was able to rely on the therapist once he allayed her fears of being found wanting by "pursuing" her with phone calls that implicitly expressed his interest in her situation and his wish to be of help. Reliance laid the groundwork for the next step, in which the therapist was able to help the patient reframe her difficulty and set her on the road to becoming a center of initiative once again.

With Mr. Jerome it was a very different story. Solipsistically fixated on a bizarre superstition, Mr. Jerome was signaling not only that he had lost the confidence that he could be adequately protected and guided but that he had lost the vital connection of kinship; he experienced himself as isolated and abandoned to fate. Only if one could bond with him would he be capable of deriving benefit from competent guidance and support. That is why, as I played out for my students how I would treat Mr. Jerome if he were my patient, I so forcefully intruded on him, insisting on my explanation in opposition to his in a way that was meant to show him I cared about him and that it mattered to me that he heard what I had to say. His internist had told him essentially the same thing I did—"Mr. Jerome, the crisis is over, your body is functioning well again"—but although he had the right words, he had the wrong music. He spoke in the calm, sincere manner that is indeed reassuring when the patient looks to the doctor as a source of strength and guidance. This was not the case with Mr. Jerome, however, so the reassurance fell on deaf—or rather, agitated—ears. By contrast, having decided that he was not even in a kinship relationship, I spoke not as one adult to another but more like a very forceful parent making a desperate effort to get something important through to a child who will not listen. That tension communicates itself and carries a caring, concerned quality that can be very effective. In my script for his therapy, my efforts at bringing Mr. Jerome into my orbit were shown to have taken hold when he could accept my explanations as helpful in orienting himself. His joining in with his "frozen pipe" analogy indicated that he was able to hear what I had to say as supportive and that fear and distress had given way to interest. It is always a hopeful sign when positive affects replace or offset negative ones. Now, to attest to the kinship bond, I showed that Mr. Jerome's preoccupation with disasters and anniversary reactions was replaced by sensible questions about how he could be certain that his physical recovery was genuine.

To show that Mr. Jerome's inability to trust had given way to reliance, I had him first refer to his internist as "My doctor" and then amend that to "my other doctor," giving me equal billing, so to speak. At that point one could begin to address his need for validation by acknowledging the legitimacy of his question and making suggestions as to how he might address those issues. I suggested to Mr. Jerome's therapist that once the patient was functioning well, he continue the validation by explicitly acknowledging, supporting, and praising the patient for his achievements. (Although the scenario of Mr. Jerome's therapy was a make-believe teaching exercise, I did not invent it out of whole cloth. The sort of interchange I have described is familiar to me from patients I have treated for post-traumatic stress disorders. Those experiences let me anticipate with some confidence what would happen with Mr. Jerome if his case were handled properly, and as we saw, his therapy essentially played itself out as predicted.)

INTEGRATING THE DEVELOPMENTAL MODEL

In the last two chapters I have introduced the five basic components of the developmental model: the sectorial view of development, the developmental spiral, the theory of affect, the hierarchical view of the positive transference, and the steps in problem solving. It is the integration of these components, however, that gives the model such power and flexibility. Let us therefore see how these different facets of development are used to organize a patient's material.

When I first meet a new patient, I hear out the patient's chief complaint. More often than not what the patient identifies as the problem is not the reason for the difficulty; consider, for example, Ms. Taft's "I am here because of Jason"—that is, "Someone other than me is responsible"—or Mr. Jerome's belief that he is panicked by the realization that he is predestined to die within a year. Rather than accepting the idea, however it is couched, that the patient is a victim, I take the chief complaint as a confused report of how that person ceased to function competently and lost a sense of self-worth. Then I identify the sector of development (see figure 1.1) in which this loss seems to have taken place. As the patient spontaneously or in response to my inquiry ranges beyond the stated reason for coming to see me, I get a broader picture of the patient's strengths and weaknesses; these too I sort out according to the sector diagram. I now have a rough picture of (1) whether the patient's difficulty is chronic or of recent origin, (2) whether there are significant difficulties not mentioned or recognized by the patient, and (3) what strengths the patient brings.

While this is happening I hear the patient's affective tone and identify the negative affect that is driving and sustaining the difficulty (see figure 2.1). I listen for any change of affect as the patient gives the history and note the content associated with that change. For example, from the way Ms. Taft's therapist's voice changed when he spoke of the satisfaction the patient got from her work, I assume that Ms. Taft's voice made a similar transition from distress to interest and joyful vitality. Such a change from negative to positive affect is further confirmation of the patient's hidden strengths, which, if one can mobilize them, can be turned to good account therapeutically.

As I sort out content and affect, I simultaneously note how the patient relates to me. Is there an implicit trust that we will get along and have something to talk about? Does the patient treat me as a helpful authority? a feared one? an adversary? a fraud? a friend? These questions give me a picture of the level of the positive transference or the difficulties with it (see figure 2.2). In Ms. Taft's case there seemed to be no obstacles in this area, but Mr. Jerome's inability to bond made reliance on the therapist an impossibility and, since without reliance there can be no therapy, that inability decided where the therapist's efforts had to be focused.

At this point I am in a good position to do some therapeutic planning. In a sense I have made myself independent of the patient's complaint. I do not have to buy into Ms. Taft's belief that her ex-boyfriend is the source of her difficulties and try to help her figure out what to do about Jason's lack of interest in her. Nor do I have to accept at face value Mr. Jerome's conviction that he is predestined to die. Instead, the question I ask myself is, Given what I know about the patient, how can I help this person restore competence and regain self-esteem?

I match the patient to the spiral of development (see figure 1.2) and, given the problem as I picture it, think of where I might best intervene. In Ms. Taft's case the most likely place seems to be at the level of decision; that is, I think her best chance at recovery is to come to realize that her depression is not due to Jason's loss of interest in her but in her putting all her eggs in the wrong basket. Her mistake is to think that someone else has dominion over her sense of worth, when her history demonstrates that she is more than capable of functioning as a competent center of initiative. Knowing that I want to try to intervene at the level of decision making, I turn to the guide for intervention (see figure 1.3) to see what I need to address and how to shape my intervention. Given her history, all that is necessary is to orient her to the idea that the relief she is intent on pursuing in the attachment sector is waiting for her in the autonomy sector. And, indeed, that proved to be a fruitful approach. The same held true for Mr. Jerome; that is, he had to be reoriented, to stop thinking of himself as a victim of fate and accept his illness for what it was. In his case, however, the patient was in the grip of a paralyzing fear that precluded a positive transference, and that situation had to be handled first, before one could see what might be done about restoring his self-esteem. In the process of forging a bond between us, I recognized the opportunity to intervene on the behavioral level of the developmental spiral; that is, I was able to make suggestions regarding exercise and monitoring his blood pressure. The patient's realization that he could regain reasonable control over his destiny was enough not only to mobilize his previously demonstrated strengths but also to further his development. He soon thereafter reflected on his goals and made a decision regarding his work that indicated his increased self-confidence.

In the clinical illustrations that follow, I further refine the application of the five basic aspects of the developmental model to the practice of brief psychotherapy. These cases will provide the reader the opportunity to think along with me and become more familiar with the model's guidelines. The more they are used, the sooner they will be integrated and become second nature.

II

Brief Psychotherapy and the Goal of Character Change

CHAPTER 3

The Patient as an Agent for Change: Bea Willingham

I PRESENT THE NEXT CASE in its entirety without comment. This will give the reader an opportunity to use the developmental model to think about why I did what I did with this patient. In the discussion that follows, I will go through the same exercise.

BEA WILLINGHAM

When Mrs. Bea Willingham first called on the telephone, she said by way of introducing herself that she wished to see a psychoanalyst and had found my name in the phone book. I suggested that she come in for a consultation.

"Bedraggled" and "slovenly" best describe Mrs. Willingham's appearance when she came for her appointment. Her hair hung limply around her face; her clothes looked as though they had been pulled willy-nilly out of a dark closet and thrown on. I noticed that her hands were grubby and that there was black dirt under her fingernails. All this seemed very much out of keeping with the refined

British accent I had heard on the phone and the obvious intelligence she demonstrated when she spoke. I was surprised to learn that she was only thirty-eight years old; had she told me she was in her fifties, I would have had no trouble believing her.

In response to my inquiry as to what had led her to call me, Mrs. Willingham told me she had recently come from England to join her husband. Married for twelve years, they were both college professors. He had been offered a good position in the Chicago area and had come to the United States alone, leaving her to finish the academic year in Britain. When she arrived here, her husband met her at the airport with the news that he had taken up with another woman—a twenty-one-year-old student in one of his classes—and asked her for a divorce. Seemingly oblivious to his cruelty, he told her that she was not welcome in his apartment and that she should find her own place to live and get a job to support herself. She had not agreed to the divorce, but she had been living alone for some months and, since a teaching job for which she had contracted was not to start until the fall, she was working in the greenhouse of a wholesale distributor of plants and flowers (she was a botanist by profession).

THERAPIST: How do you see me helping you, Mrs. Willingham?

MRS. WILLINGHAM: I am upset, very upset.

THERAPIST: Who wouldn't be in your place?

MRS. WILLINGHAM: It isn't getting any better. Up half the night, no appetite—I have to force myself to eat. I have no one to talk to. I really know no one here, and my friends are in England; I can't afford transatlantic telephone conversations.

THERAPIST: These are trying times for you. Is it so bad that you sometimes feel like killing yourself? Have you made any plans in that direction?

MRS. WILLINGHAM: Why should I do that? That would be ridiculous, wouldn't it be? I just want him to come to his senses. (*Falls silent.*)

THERAPIST: Where do I fit in? How may I be of help to you?

MRS. WILLINGHAM: (*A look of puzzlement crossing her face*) Before I was married, as an undergraduate, I had some problems and went to a psychoanalyst. He helped me a great deal. I guess I just turn in that direction when I need it.

THERAPIST: Certainly. Very understandable. And here you are.

MRS. WILLINGHAM: I see what you mean. What do I want from *you?* You can't tell me what to do, can you?

THERAPIST: That's true, but maybe we can sort some things out. It may sound like a dumb question, but why do you want your husband back? He hasn't treated you particularly well, to say the least.

MRS. WILLINGHAM: I know him. He's had a fling once before. He's not that strong; in a strange country, all alone, he wants his mummy. Of course he thinks he's in love with the first pair of arms that are ready to shelter him. I think he's just going through his mid-life crisis.

THERAPIST: But basically it was a good marriage—or not?

MRS. WILLINGHAM: It was fine. We had a lot in common; there were a lot of good things. Even in the worst times we could talk.

THERAPIST: And now he doesn't want to talk?

MRS. WILLINGHAM: He calls me once in a while. He sounds so cold on the phone, all business.

THERAPIST: You don't call him?

MRS. WILLINGHAM: I don't know. I'm scared. I think, if I call him, how am I going to compete with some fresh-faced little girl, with a firm body, who makes him feel like Superman?

THERAPIST: Sounds like your husband is not the only one having a mid-life crisis.

MRS. WILLINGHAM: Well, I . . . I just . . .

THERAPIST: You want him to come to his senses. But you seem to be behaving as if you have nothing to say about all this, as if what you've built up together over the years doesn't count, as if the bond between you gives you no leverage.

MRS. WILLINGHAM: That's how I feel.

THERAPIST: So you won't put up a fight?

MRS. WILLINGHAM: Men are such fools. She's so young . . . (*Looking down at herself*) I'm a mess, aren't I?

THERAPIST: (*Remains expectantly silent.*)

MRS. WILLINGHAM: I should get some clothes . . . do something about my hair . . . my nails. In the fall, when I start teaching, I'll have money. Right now it's a bit dicey. I didn't save much. In England salaries aren't what they are here. He paid for my ticket, but other than that I'm on my own.

Soon afterwards, our session ended. She said she would call me to schedule another appointment. She did phone some days later, saying, apologetically, that in her present financial situation she could not afford both therapy and the hairdresser and that under the circumstances she had decided on the latter.

"So you're entering the fray? The battle is joined?" I asked.

"I think I'd better, and not just give up."

"Good for you," I replied.

She did not contact me again.

Some years later, at a large cocktail party, I did not immediately recognize the cheerful, attractive lady who reintroduced herself. She had me meet her husband—there was no mention of the nature of our initial meeting—and we exchanged small talk. Since then I have had no news of her.

Now for the dissection of the case. When Mrs. Willingham presents her story, there is no way of determining whether this is going to be short- or long-term psychotherapy or whether psychoanalysis is indicated. As I listen to the story of her troubles, what impresses me and what I pay particular attention to are the strengths that she indirectly conveys in the autonomy sector of development.

She is a college professor, which tells me a great deal about her ability to undertake a long-term plan and to carry it through successfully. Although she looks disheveled and disorganized, I am impressed by the fact that though she is alone and in a strange country she has managed to find a job and is functioning independently under very difficult emotional circumstances.

What I have learned so far speaks for her strengths, her competencies. Mrs. Willingham's readiness to tell her story without reservations augurs well for reliance. The leading affect is distress and not the anger that one might expect under such circumstances. The patient's affect is under good control. But what are her incompetencies? What is undermining her self-esteem? Her outward appearance, more in keeping with a severe depression, is at odds with her well-organized narrative and general demeanor; that incongruity must be accounted for somewhere along the way. Before I can reflect on her situation and use my skills to help her, I have to be oriented to her difficulties. So I ask for clarification.

THERAPIST: How do you see me helping you, Mrs. Willingham?

By not only asking the patient to tell me about her problem but then focusing on her expectations in coming to see me, I indicate indirectly that what we will be doing together remains to be seen. Furthermore, a noncommittal inquiry like this gives me an opportunity to observe the manner in which Mrs. Willingham rises to this modest challenge, how she goes about orienting herself and establishing psychological order. Such a maneuver would not have been indicated with Mr. Jerome, who was already overwhelmed by anxiety and needed to be reassured that the therapist could help him establish coherence. In Ms. Taft's case, as it was presented, not enough was known about the patient's assets to test her organizing skills; that they were considerable was an empirical finding made later.

Mrs. Willingham's narrative, however, leads me to believe that she has the requisite strength to cope productively with the challenge of sorting out her immediate situation. If she had indicated by a significant increase in disorganization—for example, by breaking down and sobbing uncontrollably, mounting a burst of anger at me for not being sympathetic and understanding, or questioning her coming to see me in the first place—I could easily back off, acknowledge that my question was stressful, and be more forthcoming and specific in what we might do together. The latter turn of events would tell me that, as in Mr. Jerome's situation, repairing her ordering capacity would have to be the immediate focus of treatment.

MRS. WILLINGHAM: I am upset, very upset.

THERAPIST: Who wouldn't be in your place?

MRS. WILLINGHAM: It isn't getting any better. Up half the night, no appetite—I have to force myself to eat. I have no one to talk to. I really know no one here, and my friends are in England; I can't afford transatlantic telephone conversations.

THERAPIST: These are trying times for you. Is it so bad that you sometimes feel like killing yourself? Have you made any plans in that direction?

MRS. WILLINGHAM: Why should I do that? That would be ridiculous, wouldn't it be? I just want him to come to his senses. (*Falls silent.*)

When she does not answer my question as to how I might help her but replies, "I am upset, very upset," I comment that this is to be expected—acknowledging the bond forming between us and validating her—but I leave her with the task of clarifying her purpose in coming to see me. She still does not answer my original question as to what she might expect me to do for her. Instead, she lists a series of complaints that are indicative of depression—loss of appetite, insomnia, and so on. I therefore take a different tack, assuming responsibility for creating order by asking her about any suicidal plans or proclivities. If she answered in such a way that persuaded me that her depression was indeed life-threatening, I would make that concern the focus of my treatment plan, doing all I could to ensure the safety of this patient who, if suicidal, would be all alone in facing those agonizing thoughts. Given her situation, I might well insist on hospitalization. The believable reassurance that she gives me regarding this issue, however, makes me comfortable in continuing to plumb her ordering capacities to establish what might help this patient and what role I can play in that process.

I note also psychological assets in the attachment sector of development, namely the fact that she seems to have good friends, people who, if they were nearby, she could communicate with and rely upon in her present situation. I wonder to myself if that is what she might actually be looking for from me—someone to whom she can speak openly and who will help her sort out possible avenues toward resolution of her difficulties. I get an inkling that her therapy may not take as long as it might if, for instance, she were more or less exclusively dependent for emotional support on the husband who is treating her in such a cavalier fashion.

The firm pressure that I maintain as I ask her to think about what it is she wants from therapy has another motive. The patient's narrative capacity is very helpful in weaving a coherent story that clarifies both the precipitating incident of her difficulty and the assets she brings to the therapeutic task. Articulate patients, however, have a tendency to believe that in telling their story they have done their job and that the rest is up to the therapist. Therapists often cooperate with that misconception and feel challenged to figure out what to do once the problem seems to have been well delineated. I have painted myself into a corner often enough to know that I have to forestall this expectation. As the guide to intervention (see figure 1.3) makes clear, effective communication—a coherent and comprehensive narrative—is only one facet of problem solving, and it is the final step. At this point Mrs. Willingham's narrative, though indicative of her ability to organize experience on that level, should not be accepted as the background against which therapy will be conducted. Of fundamental importance in problem solving is orientation, and by that I mean a delineation of the difficulty in such a way that the patient is the central actor in the task of resolution. So far Mrs. Willingham is presenting herself as a victim who needs to be rescued. It cannot be stressed too often that this is not the job of the therapist. It is not that I do not have sympathy for what she has suffered—indeed, I am quick to acknowledge it and inwardly feel indignant about the treatment she has received at the hands of her husband—but sympathy per se will not help and can even be detrimental, if that is where our input stops. The fact is that at this point I do not know how to help her. She seems to be looking for advice. As Mr. Jerome's case illustrates, I have no objection to giving advice to a patient, but when I do it must be based on a grasp of a patient's problem and why the patient is failing to resolve it. In Mrs. Willingham's case, I do not yet have such knowledge. My thoughts about how I myself might cope under similar circumstances would be totally beside the point. Were I to introduce them, they would be an unwarranted intrusion into the therapeutic process.

Instead, my immediate goal has to be to help Mrs. Willingham clarify for both of us what she believes she is facing, so that I can think about the goal that is implicit in her orientation. In terms of the developmental spiral, how does she define competence in this situation, and what decisions follow? Then it remains to be seen whether she has the tools—the coping mechanisms—to translate her decisions into behavior that has a chance of establishing such competence and bring about self-cohesion.

Mrs. Willingham gives us a clue when, after denying suicidal intent, she says, "I just want him to come to his senses." Here she indirectly sets a goal that she has in mind and unwittingly touches on another very common issue that must be dealt with as early as possible in any therapy. It is not within my power to make her husband come to his senses. Mrs. Willingham's implicit hope that I will be able to give her the words or techniques to make this happen is very similar to that of many people who come to the therapist with complaints of being unable to form or maintain relationships. The unspoken implication is that somehow the therapist is supposed to do something about that. Here what needs to be done is to transfer the problem from the sector of attachment to the sector of autonomy; that is to say, the issue is, What are *you*, the patient, going to be able to do about what troubles you? If you have problems forming relationships, attracting people to whom you would like to be attractive, what is it that you are doing to interfere with that goal, and what can you do to make yourself more competent in that area?

It is for this reason that I continue my discussion with Mrs. Willingham in the same vein in which I began it. I focus on what it is that *she* is looking for, rather than making suggestions as to what she could do or, alternatively, essentially dismissing her complaint by suggesting that her complaint is only the tip of an iceberg and going on to ask her about the rest of her personal history, her childhood development, and so on. Implicit in the latter maneuver is the assumption not only that treatment will probably be a lengthy process but that the therapist is taking responsibility for getting at the "real" or deeper reasons for the problem.

THERAPIST: Where do I fit in? How may I be of help to you?

MRS. WILLINGHAM: (*A look of puzzlement crossing her face*) Before I was married, as an undergraduate, I had some problems and went to a psychoanalyst. He helped me a great deal. I guess I just turn in that direction when I need it.

THERAPIST: Certainly. Very understandable. And here you are.

In the above interchange, I continue to put pressure on the patient to help define my role in her therapy. At the same time, however, I continue to support her need for and request for help by mirroring or validating that aspect of her request to me. I note that I am the beneficiary of the reliance she had on her previous therapist.

Tearful children will run to their parents and expect that that contact per se will somehow solve any problem. Similarly, people often turn to therapists with the same hope. We can acknowledge the wish, but we should not accept the burden of its fulfillment. When I say, in a friendly and not a confrontational tone, "Certainly. Very understandable. And here you are," I continue to apply pressure to see if together we can arrive at a mutually satisfactory way of working on her stated goal, to get her husband to realize that divorce is not in his best interest.

> MRS. WILLINGHAM: I see what you mean. What do I want from *you?* You can't tell me what to do, can you?

Were Mrs. Willingham to become distraught, disorganized, or in any other way increasingly helpless in the face of my insisting that she focus on the hopes and wishes with which she imbues therapy, I would get a picture of incompetence that would point me in a different direction. Instead, what happens again is that, under pressure, she becomes stronger and obtains insight. Distress is now modified by interest as she finds herself altering her expectations of our relationship. Her recognition that I cannot tell her what to do, that she has to become clear as to what she wants from me if I am to help her, is a significant turn toward autonomy. In seeing herself as the center for action she has reoriented herself.

> THERAPIST: That's true, but maybe we can sort some things out. It may sound like a dumb question, but why do you want your husband back? He hasn't treated you particularly well, to say the least.
> MRS. WILLINGHAM: I know him. He's had a fling once before. He's not that strong; in a strange country, all alone, he wants his mummy. Of course he thinks he's in love with the first pair of arms that are ready to shelter him. I think he's just going through his mid-life crisis.
> THERAPIST: But basically it was a good marriage—or not?
> MRS. WILLINGHAM: It was fine. We had a lot in common; there were a lot of good things. Even in the worst times we could talk.
> THERAPIST: And now he doesn't want to talk?
> MRS. WILLINGHAM: He calls me once in a while. He sounds so cold on the phone, all business.

When Mrs. Willingham recognizes that I cannot fulfill her wish to be told what to do, she takes a very important step, one that sooner or later all patients have to take—and the sooner the better. For ultimately, once the goal is sufficiently well defined, it is the patient who either will or will not be able to do what needs to be done to reach that stated goal. Once Mrs. Willingham recognized and shouldered her responsibility, I felt able to step in and make a concrete suggestion: I would try to help her by sorting out the issues that confronted her. I began by rhetorically questioning what, if anything, she had to gain by restoring her marriage.

In Kohut's terms (Basch 1991, 1994), the patient has come into therapy with the expectation that I will fulfill an archaic selfobject function, namely, that like the parent of a distraught infant, I will take over and—as was initially necessary in the case of Mr. Jerome—will supply whatever is necessary to create order and reintegrate the self. Now she is in a position where I can offer her help on an age-appropriate level—that is, serve a mature selfobject function—by helping her to sort out the present situation and her options. It is on this level that brief psychotherapy is generally accomplished.

It quickly becomes apparent why Mrs. Willingham feels the way she does. Whatever problems the marriage has had, its rewards outweigh them. Her goal then makes good sense to me.

Given the patient's recognition that dynamic psychotherapy is a cooperative enterprise, I now have to make some decisions about how I am going to steer the process in an appropriate direction. Although I am at this point not certain that anything can be done on a short-term basis, I have gathered evidence to persuade me that nothing stands in the way. Once Mrs. Willingham understands her situation, she runs with the ball, so to speak, and that is a very promising sign for the outcome of therapy, whatever the nature of that therapy might turn out to be.

In terms of the developmental spiral, it seems to me that the most sensible place where I might intervene is at the level of decision making. As far as I can tell, Mrs. Willingham has made the unconscious decision to present herself as a helpless, hopeless creature, as if this might, in her words, bring her husband to his senses. It seems to me that, given her goal, her behavior is counterproductive and that, if anything, her way of reacting will only confirm him in his belief that he is better off with someone else. In order to further my therapeutic goal, therefore, I agree that I cannot tell her what to do but offer to help her sort things out. This addresses the decision-making level of the developmental spiral.

To refine this analysis a bit more in terms of the development of self, it seems to me that the initial period of orientation has been successfully completed and that now I am proposing that we get into the next stage of problem solving, of examining and perhaps developing new coping mechanisms. But first I need to see if her goal of reuniting with her husband makes good sense from her point of view, or whether she is focusing on it because no other avenue toward well-being has occurred to her. So I play devil's advocate and point out to her that, on the basis of what she has said, her husband might not be a particularly worthwhile life partner.

The patient rises to a spirited defense of her spouse, showing me that, in the area of attachment, she is functioning at a very high level. She has a clear grasp of her husband's weaknesses, but at the same time those problems do not vitiate the worth of the relationship, given her past experiences with him. At this point I decide that this patient could very well be helped in a brief therapy. In spite of her depression, she is able to think clearly, the goal she has in mind of reunion with her husband seems reasonable, and the problem seems to be that, in spite of her many assets, she is going about promoting a reconciliation with him in a counterproductive way. It seems to me that, in the area of decision making, she does not need any further help, and so it might make sense to examine specific behaviors as she tries to enlist my assistance in her search for competence.

THERAPIST: You don't call him?

I put this comment in the form of a question rather than a directive such as, "Why don't you call *him*, then?" or "Might it not help if you called?" The reason is that, although I have no objection to giving an advisory opinion when I think it is called for, at this point I am truly puzzled. Here is a very competent woman who does not pick up the phone. I want to learn more about what seems to me incongruous behavior. This is a situation that lends itself to a generalization about technique: Whenever things do not seem to fit in with the patient's way of adaptation, the therapist needs to establish why the disparity has occurred.

MRS. WILLINGHAM: I don't know. I'm scared. I think, if I call him, how am I going to compete with some fresh-faced little girl, with a firm body, who makes him feel like Superman?

THERAPIST: Sounds like your husband is not the only one having a mid-life crisis.

MRS. WILLINGHAM: Well, I . . . I just . . .

THERAPIST: You want him to come to his senses. But you seem to be behaving as if you have nothing to say about all this, as if what you've built up together over the years doesn't count, as if the bond between you gives you no leverage.

MRS. WILLINGHAM: That's how I feel.

The question I ask has its desired result. I now learn about the severe loss of self-esteem that Mrs. Willingham suffered when her husband's choice of a much younger woman played into her own anxieties about getting older. Behind the distress expressed about her situation is a fear that she has not faced heretofore. Her previous comment about her earlier experience with therapy and her readiness to depend on members of the psychoanalytic profession has told me that the capacity for reliance—Kohut's idealizing transference—is in place and that she is ready to rely on me for understanding, help, and support. This gives me the leverage to take the next step and indirectly reassure her that as the saying goes, looks aren't everything. But my implied reassurance—validation—that her husband would be very lucky to have her back does not carry the day, and she tells me that, indeed, she feels at a severe disadvantage when it comes to her youthful rival.

Here again I emphasize her need to make decisions and the importance of the autonomous position. Rather than saying "Poor you" or "How can we help you get a better image of yourself?" I simply ask, in a matter-of-fact fashion, whether she has decided not to try actively to bring her husband back to her. In this way I continue to reframe her problem for her. I do not dispute the fact that some very bad things have happened to her, but by placing the emphasis on "What are you doing about this?" rather than on "I wonder why this happened to you?" I am continuing to hold out the possibility that brief therapy has a chance to work here.

At this point the way has been cleared so that we can explore the stumbling block that invariably stands in the way of achieving the patient's stated aim: the actual or potential affective overload that is preventing the patient from doing what is logically necessary to deal with the immediate problem. In this case, Mrs. Willingham was being blocked by her heretofore unarticulated fear that she could not compete with a woman who had all the physical advantages of youth. Her appearance now took on an additional meaning for me. I thought she was—unconsciously, of course—letting me and the rest of the world see how she felt in comparison with her husband's girlfriend, how physically undesirable she believed herself to be.

I request clarification. Does youth really count for that much? Does the apparently satisfying bond they have built between them count for naught? That is indeed how she feels, she says.

THERAPIST: So you won't put up a fight?

Here I conclude that it is the right moment to try what obstetricians call a version, to turn the problem around so it will present differently. Mrs. Willingham initially saw herself as a victim of her husband's pathology—the suspected mid-life crisis and his infidelity—and also of her own body, which could not compete with that of his girlfriend. Understandable as her reactions are from another point of view the role of victim is not inevitable; she has accepted and adjusted herself to it. She has made an implicit decision not to fight for what she wants—and I tell her as much.

MRS. WILLINGHAM: Men are such fools. She's so young . . . (*Looking down at herself*) I'm a mess, aren't I?
THERAPIST: (*Remains expectantly silent.*)
MRS. WILLINGHAM: I should get some clothes . . . do something about my hair . . . my nails. In the fall, when I start teaching, I'll have money. Right now it's a bit dicey. I didn't save much. In England salaries aren't what they are here. He paid for my ticket, but other than that I'm on my own.

Mrs. Willingham's immediate reaction to my implicit suggestion that she has chosen to be passive and that she can actively strive toward her goal is to reiterate her role as one beleaguered. But then she has an epiphany. She looks at herself with different eyes. Her appearance fits the role of victim perfectly, but, if she has an obligation to herself to alter the situation, she has to rethink what she is about.

On the basis of her altered orientation, she begins to plan—that is, makes decisions—to change her behavior. I think that, given her reliance on me, my implicit continued confidence in her abilities has served to affirm her sense of self sufficiently to permit her to step back and look at her situation from a different angle.

> Soon afterwards, our session ended. She said she would call me to schedule another appointment. She did phone some days later, saying, apologetically, that in her present financial situation she could not afford both therapy and the hairdresser and that under the circumstances she had decided on the latter.
> "So you're entering the fray? The battle is joined?" I asked.
> "I think I'd better, and not just give up."
> "Good for you," I replied.
> She did not contact me again.

Once her perception of herself changes, the remobilization of her assets follows, and my input is no longer needed. I do, however, take the opportunity to validate her decision by voicing my admiring approval.

I have learned over the years that once a basically well-functioning person can reframe a problem—that is, get a different orientation regarding the situation—the developmental spiral in that area is activated and runs its course without necessitating further intervention from the therapist. So Mrs. Willingham, having defined competence in her present situation as ousting the rival for her husband's affection, dramatically but not unexpectedly showed herself quite capable of reflecting productively on her problem, coming to a decision, and implementing it.

> Some years later, at a large cocktail party, I did not immediately recognize the cheerful, attractive lady who reintroduced herself. She had me meet her husband—there was no mention of the nature of our initial meeting—and we exchanged small talk. Since then I have had no news of her.

I should add one more point about setting goals for therapy. At the time Mrs. Willingham left therapy, her ostensible goal of having her husband "come to his senses" had not been realized. From the developmental point of view, however, her treatment was a success. The therapist's ultimate goal is always to help the patient achieve competence and restore self-respect. In seizing the initiative to plan a course of action, Mrs. Willingham accomplished a real victory over herself as a helpless, hapless victim. That she later was indeed reunited with her husband was incidental to that achievement. As long as she took responsibility for her life, she would have come out all right regardless of what happened to the relationship with her husband.

Mrs. Willingham's case is an excellent example of how important it is for the therapist to set a goal for therapy rather than drifting and letting the patient's associations and other circumstances determine it. I do not mean, however, that we should come to premature closure on the basis of either our therapeutic predilections or snap judgments made on the basis of first impressions. For example, an analyst might very well have decided upon hearing Mrs. Willingham's complaint that a lengthy exploration of the patient's relationships generally was called for, that her complaint about her husband was the tip of an iceberg that needed to be more fully explored. A psychiatrist experienced in psychopharmacologic treatment might have focused on the patient's obvious vegetative signs of depression and prescribed medication for symptom relief. A therapist in a managed care setting in which a patient was allowed only a few sessions could well have decided to combine medication with behavioral modification, giving advice geared to helping the patient adapt to her new role as a rejected spouse.

All these approaches would have been in error. Only as the patient's complaint was evaluated in the context of the assets she brought to the therapy was it possible to arrive at a decision that made sense for this particular person. When I contrasted the patient's developmental assets with her difficulties, it became clear to me that there was an incongruity between her capabilities and her behavior. So I felt comfortable in continuing to question what she was here for until the hidden piece of the puzzle emerged, namely, her loss of self-esteem as she compared herself physically against her younger rival. It turned out that my orienting her to this issue let everything else fall into place. She herself decided on the coping mechanisms she would employ to deal with the situation, reflected upon her decision, and told me about it. She did not need my validation for her plan—she had made up her mind—but she got my reinforcement anyway; I certainly did not think it would hurt to add my *Amen.* Had she demonstrated in the interview that her present situation was only one example of a developmental deficit that precluded reasonable relationships, however, or that there was some underlying conflict that kept her from making the most of her assets, then my approach would have had to be different, and short-term therapy most likely would not have been effective.

As the case of Mrs. Willingham demonstrates, the process of establishing what the patient is there to accomplish is in itself therapeutic. Indeed, in her case, it turned out to be curative, but that was coincidental; it was not my hope, much less my intention, to have her therapy resolve itself so quickly.

I should also emphasize that goal setting with, by, or for the patient is not simply based on either the patient's wishes or what the therapist intuits about the patient's predicament. In a meaningful dialogue between patient and therapist as they negotiate the therapeutic situation, nothing is cut and dried. What the patient says may confront us with several possibilities, and we are constantly deciding what we will take as figure and what will be background—that is, what we will pursue and what we let go without further comment, at least for the moment.

For example, after Mrs. Willingham outlined her predicament and essentially summed up her aim as wanting her husband to come to his senses, I had to make a decision either (1) to say nothing and wait for her to continue; (2) to suggest that she expand on that statement, perhaps talking more about the marital relationship; or (3) to accept her goal-oriented statement and clarify how our relationship might be used in its implementation. I chose to take the latter position. Then, thinking about what I had said, the patient associated her calling me with the benefits she had derived from therapy on a previous occasion. Why not encourage her then and there to talk further about both the problems she had surmounted and what she experienced and learned in her earlier treatment? I chose not to do that and instead simply supported her looking to therapy for help now and focused her once again on how therapy and I, as her therapist, might be of use to her at this point. Again I had to choose which road to take when, having told me only that it made sense to her to maintain her marriage in spite of her husband's present behavior, she complained of his seeming indifference to her, expressed in his infrequent and then only cold, businesslike phone calls. It certainly occurred to me that I could ask questions that would lead her to explore her reaction to this callous abandonment. Were there any similarities between what was happening to her now and the problem that had led her to seek treatment when she was in college? What was her childhood like? Had she previously experienced abandonment, and if so how had she dealt with it? All were potentially worthwhile avenues into which I might have guided the patient's associations. What I did, however, in response to Mrs. Willingham's complaint regarding her husband's infrequent calls, was to ask, "You don't call him?"

Why did I make the decision I did? Mrs. Willingham presented herself as regressed and helpless, and rather than encouraging a further retreat into rumination, I wanted to see if, when challenged, she could regain control over her life and in so doing substitute hope for resignation.

Would I have taken a different tack, and would our interchange have sounded different, if she had indicated that she wanted no part of her husband after what he had done to her but was fearful about her ability to go it alone? Or would my interventions have been influenced had she decided that her husband's behavior only underscored the disgusting superficiality of men and that she was not about to demean herself by competing for anyone's affections on the level of physical appearance and dress? Of course. Any variation in anything Mrs. Willingham told me would have affected my transaction with her. But no matter what she said and what turn our discourse took, I would have kept the developmental model in mind and focused on her inability to take charge of and guide her life and what I might be able to do to help her with that problem.

CHAPTER 4

Correcting a Developmental Deficit: Warren Dale, Jr.

PSYCHODYNAMICS SEEKS to explain how and why people make the decisions that lead to behavior. Every decision is mobilized by affect and carries an affective tag. From that perspective psychotherapy is seen as a way of assisting patients to gain or regain appropriate control over their affective lives (Basch 1988).

The equanimity Mrs. Willingham displayed vis-à-vis her husband and her marriage leads me to think that she has developed a wide, well-nuanced range of affect. That is why, though she was understandably traumatized by the insensitivity of her husband, she was able to regain composure and direction with a minimum of psychotherapeutic help. More often than not, the people who come to us cannot be assumed to possess this level of maturity. Their affective development has been significantly damaged or arrested early in life, and the cure for what ails them involves undoing and correcting as much as possible of the deficiencies and distortions of that development.

The treatment of Denise Taft, Ralph Jerome, and Bea Willingham involved helping these patients regain affective control. I have noted that during my diagnostic interviews, as I listen to patients' problems with one ear the other ear is picking up their strengths. I am especially alert to their ability to manage their feelings and emotions successfully. When hearing our first three patients' stories, I was impressed by how well they had done, in spite of the difficulties in their lives, to make the best of their situations and to retain an affective flexibility in those sectors of development not directly impinged upon by their difficulties. That flexibility is a therapist's ally and often makes it possible to obtain significant change for the better in a short period of time.

There are many patients, however, with whom it becomes clear that whatever circumstances may be the focus of their chief complaint, the more basic problem is their inability to titrate their affective responses appropriately. Where affect is concerned, they may be either too labile or too restricted. They may therefore lack the capacity to orient themselves to a given situation, develop reasonable coping strategies to deal with it, recruit validating responses from others, reflect successfully on their plans and behavior, and/or seek helpful input from others by presenting their dilemma in an informative and emotionally nonthreatening manner. In other words, problem solving relies on our ability to avoid being affectively overwhelmed as we seek a solution.

The classic cases in which affective disorganization is symptomatically defended against are attachment disorders (of which the so-called narcissistic personality disorder is a subset [Basch 1988]). Since Heinz Kohut discovered—or, perhaps more accurately, uncovered—and named the selfobject transferences, therapists have had dramatic success in helping these patients psychoanalytically or in long-term dynamic psychotherapy. It would be wrong, however, as the following case illustrates, to assume that deep-seated affective limitations necessarily mandate a lengthy course of therapy and that brief therapy cannot be successful.

WARREN DALE, JR.

SESSION 1

THERAPIST: Hello, Mr. Junior.

PATIENT: My name is Warren Dale. "Junior" is an adjective differentiating me from my father.

THERAPIST: Oh, I'm so sorry.

MR. DALE: That's all right. I'm used to it—happens all the time.

I first felt ashamed at my mistake, but then there was a flash of resentment. On the phone, I had distinctly heard him say "Warrendale Junior," as if his first name and surname were one and "Junior" his last name. Usually people whose names include Sr., Jr., III, and so on, do not announce that fact upon introducing themselves; one learns about such designators from a business card, letterhead, or check. My resentment fading, I filed this bit of Mr. Dale's behavior for future reference.

One fallacy often heard in the field of therapy today is the notion that any affective reaction of the therapist to the patient's material is countertransference and, as such, undesirable. Freud was very specific that countertransference is an aspect of the therapist's unanalyzed conflicts stirred up by the patient's transference. *Unconscious* really does mean unconscious: outside of and not available to self-awareness. We as therapists can know nothing directly about our own countertransferential responses. When we are aware of having emotional reactions—positive or negative—to our patients, these reactions by the very fact of being conscious are not countertransference and should not be thought of as either pathological or necessarily problematic. Our affective responses to the patient at any given time can tell us something about our own sensitivities and about the patient's conscious and unconscious motives in trying to promote certain reactions within us; both kinds of information are important for the conduct of therapy. What is required is that therapists be as aware as possible of their emotional responses and use them in the interest of their patients rather than reacting as one might, for example, in a social situation. Accordingly, I noted and filed away Mr. Dale's effect on me and wondered whether I was dealing here with someone who used a self-protective "attack other" defense, a "Do unto others before they do unto you" way of dealing with a chronic sense of shame (Nathanson 1992).

Once we got started, Mr. Dale told me that at the age of thirty-eight, after a meteoric rise in his company, he had become second in command of the company's European operations. Yet he felt that he had no confidence in himself and became anxious about anything other than technical issues. Interpersonally, he experienced himself at a disadvantage. In social gatherings he said he had no ability to make small talk. Even at work he had problems, except in one-on-one interactions; any kind of group made him nervous. He hated conflict, or the possibility of conflict, and so could not comfortably debate a point of contention. Public speaking gave him a lot of trouble; indeed, he was referred to me because the medication prescribed to control his performance anxiety had not been effective.

As I always do, I asked him to tell me more about the specific nature of his work and to give me some examples illustrating his difficulties. It quickly became apparent that he was perfectly competent, indeed excellent, at everything he claimed he could not do. In the examples he gave me, he described business trips all over Europe in which he spent a few days at each corporate site, continually involved in negotiations, finding the middle road, and getting what would otherwise have been warring factions to work together for the corporate good. He was often in the position of the go-between who sold the branch offices on new policies and plans from headquarters. This role necessitated public speaking, addressing dozens—sometimes hundreds—of people at a time, as well as cementing business friendships over lunches and at parties. Here was a discrepancy that needed to be explained; the patient's complaints did not hold up when exposed to the light of day. Mr. Dale's narrative, incidentally, highlights the importance of not simply accepting patients' abstract and general statements of their difficulties as adequate summaries of their situations. We can learn a great deal more by eliciting specific, detailed examples that will clarify what is supposedly troubling the patient.

While I was listening, I was also organizing provisionally what Mr. Dale was telling me according to the model of the developmental spiral (figure 1.2). The situation as it stacked up so far looked quite different from Mrs. Willingham's. In her case, the failure to behave in ways that would favor competence and support self-esteem were only too obvious and made her distress very understandable. Mr. Dale's was a situation that, in my experience, is not uncommon in successful professional people and executives. Their high-level functioning attests to the acuity of their decision making and the efficacy of their behavior, but they fail to translate their competent achievement into a solid self-esteem. Their success does not bring them a sense of fulfillment.

This discrepancy between Mr. Dale's ostensible complaint and the reality of his achievement left open the reason for his seeking help and the provisional goal I might set for therapy. This sort of experience underscores the fact that the steps one takes in problem solving are no different for the therapist than they are for the patient; orientation as to what needs to be dealt with is essential for both (figure 1.3).

I let Mr. Dale know that I was puzzled; he seemed to be in fact successful where he felt he was lacking. It was the inability to enjoy his success that seemed to me to be the problem. Mr. Dale disagreed. He suggested that perhaps as long as he was in Europe things went better for him. When he was speaking a foreign language, he actually felt more comfortable. He did not think about himself; it was as if someone other than he were in his body. He told me about his affinity for languages. Besides English he spoke six languages fluently. Once on a train trip of several days' duration he became acquainted with a fellow passenger who spoke only Spanish. By the end of the journey, Mr. Dale was able to speak passable Spanish, and with the aid of a book he completed his mastery of that tongue. He would have been happier staying overseas, but he had been called back to the States to take on even bigger responsibilities, and he felt he could not refuse the promotion. Here at home, he felt ill at ease. Exploring further, I heard nothing about the way he was carrying out his duties that led me to think he was doing anything but a superb job. Here, too, he was involved in many meetings, constantly arbitrating and negotiating between various interests, so his complaint still did not make sense and did not, at least at this point, lend itself to formulating a goal for therapy.

Of course, while I was trying to figure out what was wrong with the patient, I was collecting a great deal of information on his assets. He was obviously a gifted, brilliant, and accomplished person. I was also impressed by his open, nonevasive way of talking about himself, and I contrasted this feeling with my initial impression that a sense of chronic shame might be an issue here.

In connection with telling me about the pressured pace at which he was working, he rather casually mentioned that he had bought a house in a nearby suburb but went there only on weekends. He used the company apartment in town the rest of the time, to eliminate the commute and let him be at work early in the morning—five o'clock, if not before. "And who is in the house?" I wanted to know. He seemed genuinely surprised that I would ask. After all, what did that have to do with what he came for? But he answered, pleasantly enough, that his wife and his son lived there. And since I seemed to be interested in that sort of thing, he added that he was trying to decide whether or not to get a divorce so that he might marry his current girlfriend, a colleague he had met overseas. This was said in a voice so bland and matter-of-fact that he might as well have been talking about changing barbers. I got a chill down my spine, but in the same instant I realized that Mr. Dale might well have handed me the key to understanding his seemingly unfounded complaint.

In developmental terms, Mr. Dale located his anxiety in the sector of autonomy (figure 1.1), represented by getting up to the podium and facing the world alone or inserting himself in a conflict as a middleman and resolving it. I did not see any obvious problem there but was now much more interested in the affective deficit in the sector of attachment. What was going on here that he could talk so casually about shedding a wife and a child?

THERAPIST: Is this your first marriage?

MR. DALE: No, my second. The first time doesn't really count. I got a girl pregnant in college, and she wouldn't consider abortion. So I agreed to marry her to give the baby a name, but we agreed to divorce thereafter. We knew we weren't meant to live together; we argued too much. Anyhow, the baby was stillborn, and we split. We're still friends, though. She's married to a lawyer in New York. I call her once in a while, and when I'm there, we sometimes go to lunch. Her husband knows about it—no monkey business.

THERAPIST: And your present wife?

MR. DALE: I met her at the office ten years ago, and after six months or so we got married.

THERAPIST: Had you been dating others, too?

MR. DALE: Oh, sure, I always had women, but it didn't go further. I never lived with any of them.

THERAPIST: What attracted you to your wife? What let it go further with her?

MR. DALE: Actually, she was attracted to me. She made the first move. I had noticed her, of course; she was a good dresser and had a nice personality. She was on the advertising end, and she'd come to our floor for sales meetings and such, where we overlapped. In one of these meetings, we happened to be sitting next to each other. They were really giving me a hard time. I was controlling myself, listening to their garbage instead of telling them what I really felt, but it wasn't easy. All of a sudden I felt Alice taking my hand—nobody could see—under the table, and it was as if all the tension was drained off. Naturally, we started going out after that and decided to get married a few weeks later.

THERAPIST: How did it work out?

MR. DALE: It was good. Soon after we were married I got Europe, and we had a chance to go everywhere.

THERAPIST: But?

MR. DALE: I don't know, things changed after the boy was born. We just grew apart. I think she lost interest in me. She didn't want to leave Warren in Paris when I had to travel, even though we had a wonderful nanny for him. We grew apart—different priorities, I guess. She says now that we're back in the States she wants me home on weekends to fix things around the house. Other than that, she doesn't seem to care what I do with my time.

THERAPIST: How old is your son?

MR. DALE: Warren? He's about five.

THERAPIST: What's your relationship with him like?

MR. DALE: Well, I don't see him that much. He's in front of the TV a lot. When I try to play a game with him, he doesn't have patience. Of course, I don't either. I need to be doing things, accomplishing things. I can't sit still and just read, or look out the window, or take a walk when I have no place I need to go. And there are things to do in the house, especially in the first year—everybody knows that. Warren is too little yet; he only gets in the way when I have to get stuff done. He's always asking, "Do you like me, Daddy?" I tell him I do, but he keeps asking and asking, and after a while I get irritated and tell him to go to his room. It bothers me when I get mad at the kid, but I don't know what else to do.

Here I had to fight the temptation to use Mr. Dale's inability to deal with his son's distress to focus on his difficulties with affect management. That step would have been premature. Until I was satisfied that I was sufficiently oriented to both the patient's problems and his strengths, the question of where I might best intervene could not be answered. And however much I might intend to use what was going on with his son to help Mr. Dale understand himself, it was likely that he would take comments in that direction as criticism. With any patient, until I have some evidence that the positive transference is in place and the patient is able to rely on me sufficiently, the educational aspect of psychotherapy at best falls flat, at worst generates resistance. So, though I did not forget what Mr. Dale had said, I decided to move on with a more general evaluation of his situation, past and present.

THERAPIST: Have you discussed the possibility of divorce with your wife?

MR. DALE: No, I haven't made up my mind for sure. I told Grace I want to start a family with her. We love each other, but she isn't a hundred percent sure she wants to get married either.

THERAPIST: Grace is your girlfriend? How did your relationship come about?

MR. DALE: She is—rather was—part of my team over there. So we spent a lot of time together in different hotels all over. You get to know each other pretty well when you have breakfast, lunch, and dinner together often enough.

THERAPIST: Why Grace? There were other women you ran across in your travels . . .

MR. DALE: Oh, sure. The funny thing is, I never went after Grace, sexually that is—didn't let myself think of her in that way. There were other women I met that I ended up in bed with, but I wanted my team to stick strictly to business. As the leader it was up to me to set the example, and I did.

THERAPIST: So, what happened?

MR. DALE: We'd been working together about a year, when Grace made it pretty clear that she had a lot of admiration for me and that our relationship could be more than professional. I liked her a lot, too, but I put the cards on the table and told her it wasn't a good idea to become a couple within a group like ours that had to work closely together. Anyway, I knew, and she knew that I knew, that she had someone back in Paris that she was pretty serious about. But after that I think we looked at each other differently and got a lot closer, though we controlled it. If we weren't together we'd write each other on e-mail every day; we still do. She finds me interesting. That still amazes me.

When I got the offer to take the new job and the team wound down, Grace ended her relationship, and we got together. It's been really good, but now she's got some doubts about coming back here. Job-wise it might not be smart; she has a career to protect, too.

What Mr. Dale told me about his personal life confirmed me in my belief that the source of his difficulties lay in the sector of attachment, not in that of autonomy, as he initially implied by his complaint. And I thought I could detect a pattern in that area: He became attached to both his wife and his girlfriend when they went out of their way to show that they valued him. It was a kinship issue, a need to be accepted and a serious doubt that he would be. His surprise that Grace found him interesting and attractive supported my hypothesis that his sense of self-worth had been significantly impaired somewhere along the line. Unfortunately—but not unexpectedly—his son seemed to be a chip off the old block, with his "Do you like me, Daddy?" The odds were high that what troubled the little boy was a similar insecurity about whether or not he was welcomed and seen as adding value to the family constellation. I also thought, given this pattern, that Mr. Dale would first have to be able to believe that I welcomed and valued him before he could count on me to be helpful— that is, rely on me (figure 2.2).

So far Mr. Dale and I had not negotiated an agreed-upon goal for therapy. Judging from his narrative, I felt that his initial complaint was a red herring, but in the area of his personal relationships, where I detected difficulties, his matter-of-fact attitude indicated no conscious awareness of conflict or even particular interest. There was an absence of appropriate affect here that called for clarification.

At this point, Mr. Dale casually introduced a new factor. He returned to a question I had asked earlier as to whether he had discussed divorce with his wife and said that he would have to make up his mind to say something pretty soon, because he had been told that within two months he would have to move again, this time to the West Coast; he was to receive another promotion, with a munificent salary arrangement and stock options that promised to make him a multimillionaire in a relatively few years. Now would be the time to make the break with his wife. Rather than having her and his son relocate, he would let them stay in the house here, while he took an apartment in the new place.

This new information further reinforced my belief that the patient's sense of inadequacy in the sector of autonomy was unwarranted and that his anxiety probably originated in some aspect of the attachment sector. I decided to pursue this area more actively to see if there were any clues in his earlier experiences that would help me to understand what was going on and to let me decide what I might be able to do for and with him in the relatively short time left to us for therapy. Historically, what might he be able to let me know about this affective blandness? I asked him to tell me something of his early years.

Mr. Dale responded readily and without hesitation, telling me he was an only child and that he had always known that he was unwanted, an accident. His parents, both still living, were attorneys. Both mother and father were alcoholics and quarreled incessantly. The more they had to drink, the more vicious were their arguments. Involved with each other, they had little time for him and would usually leave him to be tended to by whatever nursemaid or housekeeper was on the premises at the time. Though they neglected him emotionally, his parents demanded performance and expected him to be a high achiever in school. He did excel, hoping that doing so might bring him approval, but it never did. The occasional less-than-superior grade, however, brought him harsh criticism and threats of banishment to boarding school, where, it was impressed upon him, they would know how to deal with his lazy ways.

He recalled one occasion—he was either nine or ten years old—when he had gotten a perfect set of grades, received much praise at school, and anticipated that this time he would surely please his parents. He brought his report card to the dinner table, where his mother made no comment and his father showed no interest after he had ascertained that Warren had not fallen down in any subject. The patient recalled being overwhelmed by dizziness and nausea and vomiting his dinner on the tablecloth. His disgusted parents cleaned him up and put him to bed, where he fell asleep. The next thing he knew he was standing at the top of the stairs, calling down to them repeatedly, "Aren't you glad you have me?" By that time, his mother and father were well into their cups and engaged in one of their interminable arguments. They did not hear him, and eventually he returned to bed.

As far back as he could remember, he would periodically try to intervene in his parents' quarrels and beg them to stop. But that only resulted in their both turning their anger on him. By the time he was sent to boarding school for his secondary education, he was glad to get away.

This history lent further credibility to the idea that Mr. Dale's immediate problem lay in the attachment sector of development. His parents appeared to be emotionally handicapped in that neither could express any feeling other than anger; this meant to me that they lived with a chronic affective overload that they could not deal with through verbal or other appropriate behavior. It was an encouraging sign that the patient did not give up hope as a little boy and that he recalled trying to get his parents at least to express some affection for him when he met their expectations. But that did not ensure, by any means, that he would now respond with appropriate emotions when given such an opportunity in therapy. The lack of feeling in the relationship to his wife and his inability to understand his son's needs certainly felt troublesome to me. Given the short period of time I had to treat him, I did not believe that I could even begin to dismantle a strong defense against affective experience. If, however, he could still permit himself to use the receptive ambience of a psychotherapeutic relationship to reexperience—not just recall—at least some of the vicissitudes of his longing, then I felt we had a chance to accomplish something worthwhile.

The interchange that now followed the recounting of his childhood history reassured me that there was something to work with, directly and immediately, and that I could set an implied goal for us—namely, making him acquainted and as comfortable as possible with his emotional needs.

MR. DALE: I don't know . . . something is coming up . . . like a wave of sadness . . . (*Here he sheds a few tears.*)

THERAPIST: You are sad for the little boy at the top of the stairs.

MR. DALE: (*Sobs openly.*)

THERAPIST: (*After patient dries his eyes*) I think I understand better why you came here. Although on the surface you have made a superior adjustment and achieved a great deal, success has not addressed the real issue that is troubling you. Paradoxically, the more successful you are, the less happy you become. Your achievements don't heal that hurt, just as when you got all A's and your parents would not respond with pride.

MR. DALE: I haven't thought of all that in so long.

THERAPIST: Too painful, so you put it out of your mind and accounted for what was bothering you in other ways.

MR. DALE: When I think about it, you're probably right. I do handle all sorts of conflict at work without trouble, but it's the conflict between my parents I couldn't handle. (*Mr. Dale's insight tells me that orientation has been achieved and that, as his comment shows, his intellect is now free to participate in resolving his difficulty. The blank space where affect should be has been filled in by interest, and I assume that he is now in a position to rely on me as we move forward.*)

THERAPIST: Exactly. So the point is not how you handle conflicts today, but what they remind you of—that's the problem. (*With reliance in place, my "Exactly" is not an idle interjection or an attempt to make the patient feel good about himself; it is a validation meant to strengthen the bond between us.*)

MR. DALE: What do I do with all this knowledge?

THERAPIST: Oh, that will take care of itself. Just think of all the things you learned in school. Who knows what multiplication tables and the rules of grammar will lead to when we first learn them? But eventually we manage to use them, each of us in our own way.

MR. DALE: You think it's that basic?

THERAPIST: Absolutely. What we're talking about—your emotional life—is fundamental.

MR. DALE: Why am I so tired?

THERAPIST: You're finding your way in strange country. That's always tiring.

MR. DALE: Like starting a new project with people you've not worked with before?

THERAPIST: Yes, that's what I mean.

This last part of the session was very encouraging to me. That Mr. Dale could quickly make apt analogies and relate his new experiences in therapy to familiar, previously mastered events augured well for treatment.

We accomplished a great deal in this first session: We had set a goal and were already making headway toward it as the patient became acquainted and more comfortable with his past and present feelings. I learned that once kinship was established, his affective deficit could be corrected; that is to say, the requisite affective development was in place and was defended against only by the anticipation of being misunderstood and disappointed. This situation is of course very different from the one in which it becomes clear that the patient has never been able to experience appropriate feelings (Basch 1988). In terms of problem solving, once he was oriented Mr. Dale showed that he had the skill to cope with his feelings, to reflect upon them, and to communicate them accurately and in a meaningful manner.

By the time I saw Mr. Dale, I had made it a practice to see every patient initially for a double session, an hour and a half. In the interest of exploring the patient's issues thoroughly and setting a goal, I recommend this practice even when the number of sessions is restricted. One can accomplish much more when the process of becoming acquainted with the patient and the problems does not have to be interrupted prematurely. With Mr. Dale, given his imminent departure from the city, I decided to continue in this mode, to give us every opportunity to do our work. I also thought about meeting with him more than once a week and really stepping up the intensity of therapy, but I decided against it. I felt that the patient would need more time between our meetings to let what he was experiencing in the sessions be integrated with the rest of his functioning.

SESSION 2

In the second session, Mr. Dale spontaneously spoke further about his childhood experiences. What he said substantiated my initial impression that he was raised in a home in which reasonable affection and tenderness were rarely if ever expressed or conveyed. His positive emotional response to my clarifications in the first session and his use of analogies to integrate what we were talking about with the rest of his experience let me know that he could now rely on me and accept me in a guiding supportive role.

That let me take the next step, and when the opportunity presented itself, I explained affective development to him. I described the basic process of communication that, from birth on, permits a baby to make itself understood and through which the baby, in turn, can understand the parents' mental set long before verbal speech is in place. The idea that feelings and emotions, positive and negative, arise in the process of striving for age-appropriate competence made immediate sense to him. He understood how the repeated failure to involve his parents led him to avoid the mobilization of affect and to retreat into silence and autonomous activity when there seemed to be no hope of attachment.

I now thought I understood better the confusion around his last name that had served to embarrass me when we first met. He unconsciously emphasized the "Junior" to signal that, in vital respects, he was still a little boy, looking desperately for the emotional resonance that was missing from his childhood. I kept this possible explanation of his behavior to myself. (I had altered my initial impression that perhaps Mr. Dale, in embarrassing me when we met in my waiting room, was in the habit of shaming before he could be shamed. I had doubted that interpretation anyway as I heard of his success as a manager. He did not sound like a person who leads by shaming and instilling fear in his subordinates; quite the contrary.) I did say to him that his response to women who made it clear that they wanted him might well be related to the need to have others signal their acceptance and readiness to respond emotionally so that he would not reexperience the repeated disappointment he suffered at the hands of his parents.

We talked further of his displaced fear of conflict and concluded that exposure to conflict now probably reawakened, on some level, the fear that he would lose his parents. Mr. Dale agreed; the threat of divorce was the recurring theme in his parents' arguments. He added by way of corroboration that when he had to handle disagreements today, what he dreaded was a feeling of tension in his chest and gut that accompanied his managerial activities and took away whatever pleasure he might have felt in his performance. I suggested to him that what he was experiencing was raw affect, the building blocks of feelings and emotions (Basch 1988). I pointed out that if there had been no one to respond verbally to him, he would never have learned to express himself and think in English; by the same token, his parents' inability to talk to him in the language of emotion left him handicapped in that regard. All they had available to them was anger, a severely limited affective vocabulary. Mr. Dale's response to my explanation showed that he understood very well what I was saying.

At the close of this second meeting, Mr. Dale said, "I am very satisfied with what we did today" and offered me his hand, which I shook firmly. He thus acknowledged the bond that had formed between us and attested to the fact that he indeed felt welcomed, understood, and valued.

I should add that Mr. Dale's ready understanding of what I was telling him did not depend on the fact that he was of superior intelligence. I have found that patients generally have no difficulty understanding and using didactic developmental explanations.* Such explanations narrow the distance between the therapist and the patient, who often feels unnecessarily incompetent in the expert's presence. There can be no direct transference of competence—my achievement cannot become someone else's—but by including my patients in my thinking I show them that there is no abyss that separates us and that we are not dealing with anything mysterious but rather with human experiences gone awry in some way yet to be determined. This approach not only reduces the shame that the role of patient often generates but holds out the hope of control to the patient, opens the door to competence, and creates an ambience that paves the way for the work that needs to be done. Also, as in Mr. Dale's case, this sort of discussion usually results in stimulating corroborative memories that give individual meaning to the principles outlined.

In terms of the developmental model, the success of orientation does not guarantee the next step in problem solving, the acquisition of appropriate coping mechanisms. When the requisite capacities have not been developed, it is up to the therapist to help get the patient up to speed. As John Gedo (1979, 1988) has also pointed out, insight into the origin and nature of a patient's difficulties is often not enough by itself; there are skills that one must explain—teach, if you will—to the patient. It is true that, as Freud pointed out in his papers on technique, intellectual understanding is no substitute for emotionally charged insight, but that does not mean that the intellect is put on hold while we do our therapy. This second session with Mr. Dale is a good example of the futility of artificially dividing therapy into affective (dynamic) and cognitive (educational). In teaching Mr. Dale about affective development I was not simply educating him but, like a good and effective parent, conveying my interest and concern for his welfare and continued maturation. What it comes down to is that attention to a patient's affective needs without the substance that will enhance autonomy is as ineffective as attempts to

---

*The exceptions are patients like Gerald Shellman, described in chapter 9, in whom the fear of particular affective experiences is so strong that they cannot afford even to think about such issues, lest they be overwhelmed by anxiety.

help a patient with a cognitive approach that does not take into account the relationship to the therapist and what it says about the patient's affective development.

SESSION 3

Mr. Dale opened the meeting by saying that he was more at peace with himself. On the weekend he had spent more time with his son and really looked at him. He was dismayed that little Warren—or Butch, as they called him—was so nervous and irritable. Nothing seemed to please him or to hold his attention very long. On Friday night, when the boy had a nightmare, he went to him and tried to quiet him down, but Butch screamed until his mother came to hold him. Butch woke up in terror again on Saturday night. Mr. Dale again went into the child's bedroom and this time just put him on his lap and said, "Dad loves you and is so glad you are his boy." Butch calmed down immediately and after a few minutes went back to sleep. The next day Mr. Dale noticed that Butch was much easier to get along with, and he planned an outing for the two of them, which went very well. He also noted that he himself was much less tense and could sit quietly without having to be doing something every minute. "Sounds like you learned one more language," I said.

Mr. Dale then talked about the increasing distance between his wife and himself. He again dated it to the birth of their son, when he had felt abandoned by his wife's involvement with the child. He, in turn, had withdrawn, and his wife seemed satisfied with that arrangement. He never tried to change it; he and Alice were very proud of the fact that they never argued, and he was not going to get into a cycle of accusation and recrimination, as his parents had.

I suggested that it was not only his discomfort with conflict that prevented him from doing something about his isolation from his wife after their child was born, but also the need to avoid the shame that he expected would accompany any plea for understanding from Alice—a repetition of what had happened to him in childhood. Although the incident on the stairs was a clear, poignant memory, it was undoubtedly not the only time when he was desperate for affective affirmation and was ignored. And, I explained, when one opens oneself up in the hope of a particular response and is ignored or rebuffed, the intensity of one's wish turns into shame—a painful feeling of worthlessness. When that happens often enough, one learns that reaching out will only be misunderstood or rebuffed and avoids such occasions. One stops trying to get what one so desperately needs. So Mr. Dale, anticipating that he would only be further humiliated, did not reach out to his wife. I also told him that, were it not for his intervention, his son would very likely have eventually stopped his refrain of "Do you like me, Daddy?" Having become ashamed of his need, he would withdraw from emotional contact as Mr. Dale had done. At this point Mr. Dale recalled several incidents in which his mother seems to have purposely held him up to ridicule, leading him to feel very ashamed. He related his almost fanatic perfectionism in his job to these feelings; if all contingencies were anticipated and no room for error existed, then no one could fault and shame him, and he was safe. I agreed, validating his analysis.

SESSIONS 4–6

Mr. Dale commented that he had felt afraid on the way to the session. In past days he had found himself crying in his car; he felt so alone. The whole reason for his coming to see me had changed. Nothing at work bothered him any more; what he needed to do now was to learn to be comfortable with his emotions and with emotional relationships. I agreed with him and told him that the fear he experienced coming here was understandable. He was moving rapidly into a territory that had heretofore been closed to him. The fear that what he was learning about himself might overwhelm him was perfectly understandable. In his childhood no one had helped him deal appropriately with his feelings, and so, unconsciously, he had to protect himself as much as he could from intense emotions. Therefore, the emergence of strong feelings in the therapeutic relationship could not help but be somewhat frightening. Yet he was daily demonstrating to himself both the benefit of looking at this aspect of his life and his ability to deal with it productively, so the fear would not stop him; he would continue to learn more about himself.

My emphasis here was on the continuing validation of the patient's newfound insight. Although he showed that he was able to make progress on his own, it would be a serious mistake to remain silent or noncommittal as he brought in the evidence of his achievements. I was working here on two levels: In confirming him in his reflection and self-examination I encouraged the adult Mr. Dale to continue his efforts, but my approval and obvious pleasure in his progress also targeted the child he once was, this time giving that little boy the affective feedback he needed back then. In other words, therapy was providing him with a corrective emotional experience.

"Corrective emotional experience" is usually uttered disdainfully by psychoanalytically oriented therapists. It has become equated with Franz Alexander's (1954, 1958) attempt to short-circuit the analysis of the transference by having the analyst role-play the parent the patient is believed to need. Alexander's suggestion is often made to seem ludicrous by those who seem not to have read what he actually wrote. His point was that since as a matter of course sensitive therapists find that they adapt themselves to the differing needs of their patients, this adaptation might as well be done in a considered manner. This was a good observation and not a bad suggestion; the problem was that its proper execution demanded a much greater knowledge of normal development than we had when Alexander raised the issue. Now that such knowledge is available, the corrective emotional experience requires no role-playing; the therapist need only establish the patient's developmental needs and address them appropriately. A corrective emotional experience entails more than the solution of a particular problem or the warm glow that often comes with insight; it heralds a characterologic change in depth. It is usually brought about when the therapist succeeds in being able to address simultaneously a patient's archaic and mature selfobject needs around a particular issue and meet them both effectively. This is what happened in Mr. Dale's case.

Mr. Dale's insight into his affective life and the effect it had on relationships with his family led me to believe that my evaluation of his situation had been sufficiently accurate. His incompetence lay not in the sector of autonomy but in that of attachment. The goal I set for us—helping him learn to be emotionally effective—had held up in practice, and the patient was making giant strides in that direction. Fortunately, his capacity for affective development did not seem to have been significantly harmed, and once I could frame the problem for him in a way that he could understand, he was able to use his considerable assets to deal with it productively. He could see himself in his son, and in the process of addressing the boy's affective longing, he began to heal himself.

Apart from my explanation and guidance, what made Mr. Dale's treatment progress so favorably was the use I made of the positive transference need that he displayed so clearly. I have learned over the years that the accomplished man or woman who comes into the office—self-sufficient, in control, and all business—has, just below the surface, an almost desperate longing for a trustworthy and effective parent. In other words, there is a readiness for reliance and validation that meshes with the therapist's willingness to participate actively as a mentor. As the cases that have gone before and those that follow illustrate, however, it is vital for short-term treatment that the therapist's parental and mentoring activity be directed toward the patient's progression and competence in the here and now, rather than toward regression and immersion in the vicissitudes of the patient's childhood.

Guidance—as opposed to concrete advice—is very effective in meeting the patient's need for a reliable and supportive figure. Mr. Dale's response to my moves in that direction clearly indicated that the intervention had hit the mark; he used what I had said in his own way to correct some of the difficulties that he saw in his life. His capacity to rely on me to support and guide him made it possible for me to take the next step of validating him in a meaningful way. So, when he described how he was able to help his son when the boy was disturbed by a nightmare, I commented that he seemed to have learned a new language. This is what Kohut meant by *mirroring*—or, as I prefer to call it, *validating*—the patient's emotional set.

Mirroring should not be equated with what is often referred to as "unconditional love" or "total acceptance"—an indiscriminate, simplistic catering to the patient's needs of the moment—or taking it as axiomatic that "the patient is always right" and agreeing with whatever the patient says. Rather, mirroring is an expression of a considered judgment, by a trusted figure, that one is on the right track and that one's achievements or difficulties are understood. It is this validation, whether in therapy or outside of it, that gives a person the motivation to stay on course and put forth the effort required to do so.

Mr. Dale was now working more reasonable hours and driving home after work every day. His son was responding well to the time Mr. Dale was spending with him, but not surprisingly he was still behaving like a troubled child, though less so. Observing how angry the boy could get when even mildly frustrated, Alice wondered whether it was her fault for overindulging Butch, as he was their only child. "No, it has to do with me," my patient replied.

As he committed himself to his family, investing time and effort in his home life, Mr. Dale found that his wife was becoming more like the animated, interesting person that he had married. "She looked beautiful, positively radiant, when we went to church last Sunday. I can see that it's me, not her, who created the problems between us," he said. I commented that his sensitivity to any real or perceived slight had led him to withdraw from Alice after their son's birth. Rather than sharing her investment in the baby, he automatically— that is, unconsciously—judged her interest in little Warren to be exclusive and excluding. He acted as if Alice's love for the baby, like the bond of anger between his parents, was a linkage that left no room for him.

Mr. Dale reported that he and Alice had several long talks in which he told her much of what he had learned about himself in his therapy sessions. Alice was attentive and pleased to be included. He told me that he felt as if he were falling in love with Alice all over again. "It's a different, less fragile you, one that permits himself to take more of a chance with love," I said. He was no longer thinking of divorce, and he realized he would have to end the relationship with Grace. He had had other lovers during his marital life, but now for the first time he saw that ending the relationship was not just a practical matter; it involved another person's feelings. He planned to talk to Grace and in essence tell her what had happened to him and ask for her understanding.

The patient's recognition of the part he played—or, rather, had until now failed to play—in his son's upbringing, his realization that he had a great deal to do with the distance that existed between himself and his wife, and the considerate manner in which he dealt with his separation from Grace indicated to me that Mr. Dale was capable of empathic understanding, the highest form of affect development (Basch 1983). That is to say, he was no longer disavowing his feelings, but could sufficiently step back from them to put himself in the place of the other and vicariously grasp that person's emotional experience.

Sessions 7–9

Our meetings were interrupted when the patient went to Europe for a week on business. His first comment to me when we met again was that he was very aware of having missed a session. He wondered how he would feel in a few weeks, when he moved to the West Coast. He did not want to talk to any other therapist. Could he call me on the phone if he needed to do so? I said that would be fine.

Had Mr. Dale not brought up the fact that our treatment was drawing to a close, I would have introduced the subject. Perhaps I would have said something to the effect that our work had gone well and that he had acquired not only an understanding of how his past had influenced his present behavior but a set of psychological tools that would enable him to use that knowledge productively after our sessions came to an end. Then I would have waited to hear his response, to see where this would have led.

As with any other aspect of developmental therapy, there is not a standard formula that can guide the therapist in handling the end of treatment. Especially when both patient and therapist may feel that extraneous circumstances are forcing the issue, I tend to be very flexible and to go along with the patient in fashioning the termination. That is, I am agreeable to maintaining contact through letters, phone calls, or an occasional meeting when the latter is feasible.

Mr. Dale went on to tell me that while he was in Paris, he met with Grace and told her of his plan to stay with his wife and son, elaborating how this decision had evolved. Instead of shying away from her initially dismayed and then sad emotional response, he used his expanded grasp of emotional life to see her through her disappointment and was able to console her. They parted as friends. He noted that even though he was under stress, he did not drink too much. He then told me something I had not known before: In the past he regularly drank three or four martinis every night, and more when he was under pressure. Now he still liked a glass of wine with his dinner, and that seemed to satisfy him. We discussed that what he had been trying to dissolve with alcohol were emotional tensions; now that he had words for his experiences and could reflect on them, he did not need to drown them.

At home, he continued to observe himself behaving most uncharacteristically. For instance, when Butch accidentally let their collie out of the yard, he just laughed and made finding the dog an adventure for the two of them. Not so long ago, something like that would have sent him into a fury. He noted that both his son and he were quieting down; they were able to relax and were not so irritable with each other. The "Do you like me?" had ceased.

As I did with Mr. Dale, I have many times used my knowledge of affect development to open up this area of development for patients. Rather than waiting for therapy to make up for past affective deprivations or misunderstandings, patients often find that they can speed the process by doing for others—especially their children, but sometimes their spouse or associates—what had not been done for them. Indeed, the doing can be more effective than the receiving. The fact of the matter is that the therapist can never make up, point for point, for what has been missed in childhood. A therapist's regressive attempt at what in German is called *wiedergutmachen*—making everything good again—will inevitably fail. No matter how much one can give a patient in the way of affective feedback, the adult patient is no longer the deprived child. Patients often complain that what they are receiving is never enough; something is always "missing." Giving what one once needed seems to be as close as one can get to a substitution or making it up to oneself. The problem was that until I learned to guide the patient actively, it could take a long time before trial and error let us inadvertently stumble on the answer. Knowing what we now do about affect development makes it much less a hit-or-miss proposition.

In his last session, Mr. Dale chose to review the course of his therapy. What impressed him most, he said, was my interpretation that the reason he dreaded conflict was that it reawoke or threatened to reawaken his fear of losing his parents. He told me of several recent business confrontations in which he did what had to be done without experiencing inner turmoil. He felt he had come to grips with that anxiety by facing his past, a past that saddened him but that he could now separate from the present. We parted on that note. Two months later I received a call from him in which he said he was doing well and was working on the issues we had discussed. A brief note at Christmas, which I acknowledged with a letter, confirmed his continuing progress.

Even if Mr. Dale's treatment had not been artificially limited by his move, it probably would not have lasted much longer. As long as one does not preclude brief psychotherapy by stressing issues that would take a long time to resolve and by underestimating the patient's ability to contribute to recovery, one will often be pleasantly surprised by the momentum given to the process by the patient. Many patients like Mr. Dale, once oriented to their situation, mobilize capacities that either were not obvious before or were operating only in other sectors of development.

People like Mr. Dale are classified as having narcissistic personality disorders; their grandiose, often demanding and self-centered attitude and/or behavior suggests the legendary Narcissus, who fell in love with his reflection to the exclusion of everything else. The psychological facts are, of course, quite the opposite. When so-called narcissistic individuals become patients, their grandiosity is soon seen to be a failed attempt at shoring up an overwhelming insecurity about their self-worth—the very opposite of self-love. In any case, it is important that one's interventions be guided by the developmental model rather than by the particular designator we are called upon to use for statistical or insurance purposes.

The next patient to be described, Mr. Cain, would also be labeled narcissistic. The contrast between Mr. Cain and Mr. Dale highlights the problem of diagnostic labels when it comes to formulating a treatment plan. The assets that each patient brings, each one's particular manner of problem solving, and the patterns of affect management each has developed, even if only marginally different—and usually they are highly idiosyncratic—mandate radically different psychotherapeutic strategies.

CHAPTER 5

Shame and the Restoration of Self-Esteem: Jacob Cain

I N ALL PSYCHOTHERAPY, the emotion of shame is a frequent issue. Its unrecognized presence often prolongs therapy unnecessarily, playing a dual role: shame may be the source of the patient's difficulty, while at the same time the fear of being shamed prevents the patient from being open with the therapist. But it is not only our patients who are rendered unnecessarily incompetent by this basic affect turned sour. I see it often in my teaching. I finish my presentation and ask for questions and comments. Immediately twenty pairs of eyes, which up to that point had been focused on me, drop. There is a sudden interest in the arms of a chair, or fingernails, or the design of the carpet. No one says a word; the students' discomfort is palpable. It does not bother me, because I expect their reaction.

As I said earlier, affect drives behavior, and shame—present, anticipated, or feared—is the affect that is ever-present in our culture (Nathanson 1992). In and of itself, shame is not at all a bad thing; it is its misuse that makes for trouble. We are first and foremost social animals. To get the benefits of kinship, to be a welcome group member, one must learn the rules that define acceptability. Shame sends a signal that a particular course of conduct is unacceptable and that any hope of gaining approval through it is doomed to disappointment. So, one-year-old Baby Alan, accustomed to the smiles and delighted comments of his parents when he shows interest in his surroundings, is suddenly confronted with his mother's harsh, disapproving tone and the disturbed expression on her face when he has become interested in the bowel movement in his diaper. Alan's expectation that his efforts at painting his crib with this intriguing stuff will be met with delight is disappointed and is replaced by the pain of rejection. Who can relate to a face like that? His eyes drop, his head hangs down, and the anticipation of shared excitement is converted into the familiar dilatation of facial blood vessels that, in an adult, signal embarrassment. Contact between his mother's eyes and his is broken, and, as tension mounts, a pitiful cry signals the baby's distress. Let us hope that Alan's mother's tone softens and that, as she begins to clean up the mess, she conveys by her behavior that it is not the little boy but only what he did that is distasteful to her.

I think of the affects of shame and interest as functioning like a traffic light on the road to competence and self-esteem. Interest is the green light that tells us we should go ahead, that the possibility of performing competently is definitely there. Shame, like a red light, tells us that we ought to stop and reevaluate the situation, that something is wrong. When it functions effectively, shame prevents our continuing on a course that appears guaranteed to undermine kinship and the search for acceptance and social competence. Unfortunately, and not uncommonly, the sense of worthlessness that is the hallmark of shame becomes attached not just to the offending deed but to the person shamed, whether because of the vulnerability of the infant, the frustration, insensitivity, or anxiety of the caregivers, or some combination of these factors. It is not surprising, then, that the most common phobia is the fear of public speaking. Calling attention to oneself once again is more than can be expected of anyone who has been shamed too often early on.

Before I understood what was happening, I used to suffer greatly when students did not seem interested, much less excited, by my presentations. I felt that I had failed, and I was shamed by my failure. My expectation of a response—and not necessarily one of agreement—was disappointed. I must not have said anything worthy of further discussion. As I learned about affect theory, however, I realized that I was not the only one in the room who was ashamed. The downcast eyes and hanging heads of my audience were not indicators of bore-dom but rather the visible signs of a collective shame reaction—in this case, the fear of being found wanting by the teacher and, in the process, shamed. I had been cast willy-nilly in the role of the parental authority, waiting for an opportunity to show each of them that I knew and they did not, that I was competent and they incompetent, that I was worthy and they worthless. What to do?

Shame is disorganizing. For a time, the person who has been shamed or fears shame loses some degree of command over the cop-ing skills acquired through previous experience. Therefore, to try to force the issue with my reluctant audience would be a mistake. Calling on someone in the group to speak up would only reinforce the very sense of shame that I needed to mitigate as the student coerced into contributing stumbled and stuttered and, in the process, discom-fited the others. My initial temptation to retaliate and make those I blamed for my failure ashamed in turn—for example, by attacking them for their passivity—would be counterproductive and would only lead to an escalation that transformed shame into anger all around. A better idea has been to show the students that they are not in danger, that the fear that they will be shamed is groundless. Comments that are geared to accentuate kinship take me out of the negative parental role sufficiently to let one or two members of the audience contribute:

"Have any of you had a case like my Miss So-and-So?"

"I'm not so sure I got such-and-such a point across. Did I make it rea-sonably clear?"

"I'd be interested if this-or-that concept is something you've heard about before, perhaps in different terms."

Since I react positively and do not shame the students by respond-ing either defensively or superciliously to whatever they might say, the tension in the room abates sufficiently to let them generate what is often a very interesting and profitable discussion for all of us.

My experience as lecturer and seminar leader highlights the ubiq-uity of shame in our society. Here are highly accomplished people who have earned professional and graduate degrees and who, in the-ory, have every reason to be confident and secure in their self-worth. Nevertheless, they behave as if in calling attention to themselves they put themselves in danger of being exposed as unfit, stupid, a laugh-ingstock. If shame or the potential for being shamed turns out to be the constant companion of even highly functioning individuals in a profession dedicated to understanding human emotions, then it is not surprising that shame can play such a pivotal role in our patients' lives.

Donald Nathanson (1992) describes four defensive reactions avail-able for dealing with this dreaded affect: *withdrawal, attack self, attack other,* and *avoidance.* Together they make up what he calls the *compass of shame:* The first three of these reactions are self-explanatory. The fourth, avoidance, designates those adaptations that use the fear of shame as a motivator for competent functioning. So, for example, a person who is chronically shy, convinced that no one is really inter-ested in hearing what he has to say, might go to the other extreme and write books about psychotherapy. Avoidance mechanisms—"reaction formations" in psychoanalese—head off or compensate for shame and shyness. "We try harder" is not the motto of Avis Rent A Car alone.

Sometimes it is evident from the beginning of therapy that a perva-sive sense of shame is creating a self-esteem problem. Paradoxically, however, as the following case illustrates, many patients cannot bring the nature and origin of the shame to light until the therapist recog-nizes the presence of shame and takes steps to counteract it.

JACOB CAIN

Session 1

Jacob Cain, a forty-five-year-old married real-estate salesman, came to see me at his wife's insistence. She had told him that his constant faultfinding, arguing, and attempts to manage every detail of the fam-ily's life were becoming intolerable, and she was threatening to seek a divorce if he could not learn to control himself. Mr. Cain felt that he was being discriminated against because he was a man; in an other-wise all-female household, no one wanted to listen to him. As far as he was concerned, he was only doing his best to participate in raising his three daughters. But neither they nor his wife nor her mother, who lived with them, had any use for his opinions. Actually, he said, he himself had for some time considered seeing a therapist about his disappointing home life and thought he could profit from some discussion with me. As he put it: "I anticipate that the application of your expertise to the matter of my cogitation may well redound in a benefit to my psychological well-being." He was a man who did not go swimming but rather "perambulated to the natatorium."

This awkward attempt at erudition made me feel sad even as I noted that there seemed to be no immediate obstacles to kinship and reliance. I had an urge, which I contained, to say to him, "Don't try so hard, it's not working." Indeed, his wordiness had the opposite effect of what he intended. As I listened to him, a scene that I had not thought about for decades came to mind. I was on a bus, sitting behind an elderly, poorly dressed couple. In voices meant to be heard by the other passengers, they were discussing the grand gifts of house and furnishings they were making to their newly married son and his wife, the Cadillac they had on order for themselves, and so on. I felt embarrassed for them.

It seemed to me that Mr. Cain was doing a poor job of warding off a sense of inferiority and its attendant shame. Tentatively I set myself the goal of establishing the source of his insecurity. What perceived incompetence had led him to this ludicrous attempt at shame avoidance?

Mr. Cain, seeking to show me how he was misunderstood, described an argument that had taken place the night before. His eldest child, aged fourteen, had come home from school with what Mr. Cain considered to be unrealistic, ultraliberal ideas regarding income distribution and the reasons for poverty. Since he knew from experience what it was to be poor and had risen to comfortable wealth, he felt he had something to say about the subject. But nobody wanted to listen to him. His daughter stomped off to her room in tears, and his wife took her side, telling him, "Talk *this* over with the psychiatrist when you see him tomorrow." I felt encouraged by the patient's capacity for reflection and narrative; he apparently realized that in order to understand his experience I would have to hear specifics. Had he not volunteered an appropriate example, I would of course have asked him to give me one.

MR. CAIN: What do you think, Doctor?

THERAPIST: Well, I've never yet won an argument with a fourteen-year-old; I'm not surprised by what happened. (*Here the patient gives a little smile, which I take to be an encouraging sign. A capacity for humor at one's own expense is evidence of the ability to step outside oneself and look at one's behavior through another's eyes. It enhances the effectiveness of the clarifications, interpretations, and confrontations in psychotherapy.*)

MR. CAIN: (*In a more relaxed tone and with less need for four-syllable words*) What do you do in these circumstances? How do you handle such situations?

THERAPIST: I think it's a matter of respect . . .

MR. CAIN: (*Interrupting excitedly*) That's it exactly. The lack of respect. They say I criticize them. *They* criticize *me!* In my house a man gets no respect. But I pay for everything. We disburse more in a month—no, in a week—than my parents expended in a year. The income flow that supports their life-style is generated by me; where is the respect?

THERAPIST: What I was going to say, in response to your question as to how I might handle a teenager's instructing me about the ways of the world, is to pay less attention to the content and more to her need to be given a respectful hearing. Usually one does not have to agree or disagree with what is said. It is taken for granted that a parent's views are outmoded. (*Here I do not validate—that is, look at and support—what happened from the patient's point of view. To the contrary, I invalidate his position in a confrontational manner. I intend not so much to educate him as to see how fixed he is in his attitude, and how he will react to a dissenting voice.*)

MR. CAIN: Well, I want a hearing also. Even the eight-year-old countermands my instructions, and my wife sides with her.

THERAPIST: For example?

MR. CAIN: She left her bicycle in the driveway again, and I told her as punishment she would have to stay home all weekend. But her mother drove her to a birthday party on Sunday anyway. When I was a stripling, my father's word was law.

THERAPIST: Tell me about that. (*Feeling I have learned as much as I am going to for the moment about the tensions in his home life, I use the mention of his father to detour into his childhood history, not to establish an explanation for his troubles but to learn something about what has gone right and what has gone wrong for Mr. Cain over the years.*)

MR. CAIN: We were impecunious. My father survived the Holocaust and came here with nothing. He worked for a tailor and eventually married his employer's youngest offspring—my mother. The shop could barely support one family, to say nothing of two.

The story of Jacob Cain's childhood was one of deprivation and anxiety. He heard constant discussions about the lack of money; as his three siblings came along, the need for ever-stricter economy was an ongoing topic. For example, he remembered that toilet tissue was an unheard-of luxury. Old newspapers, cut into squares, served that purpose. In the bathroom there hung only one large towel, which was shared by all members of the family. It was changed, at best, once weekly.

His father had persuaded himself that he had a bad heart, and from early on he impressed Jacob with the responsibility the boy would have for the family when—not if—the father died. As far as Jacob could recall, the fear that his father would die was a constant companion throughout his childhood. The need to apply himself, to work hard, and to forgo activities that brought no income was dinned into him. His mother, perhaps a bit slow mentally, also lived in terror of her husband's prophesied demise and could only echo his admonitions when Jacob looked to her for understanding or reassurance.

Although Jacob lived with chronic anxiety, he never doubted that his parents loved him. Nor did he resent a childhood that found him running straight home from school to help out in the shop or care for the younger children. It was just a given that play was for others and not for him. He felt very close to his father and admired his grit in the face of adversity. The family occupied two rooms behind the shop, and many nights Jacob would wake up from a bad dream to hear the whirring of the sewing machine as his father worked into the morning hours to finish an order. The sounds indicating that his father was still alive and busy comforted him and let him go back to sleep.

When Jacob was sixteen, his father did indeed die, not of heart disease but of a fulminating leukemia. In his last days he impressed on Jacob that he was now the head of the household and repeatedly made him promise to be responsible for supporting his mother and his younger brothers and sister.

A few years earlier, his father's draconian frugality had enabled him to make a down payment on the three-story building in which the tailor shop occupied the ground floor. Jacob, from the age of fourteen, was assigned the maintenance of the building; that work was considered to be too strenuous for his father to undertake. After his father's death, Jacob continued to service the apartments, which produced rental income to support the family and pay the mortgage. A retired tailor, a widower who had found time hanging heavy on his hands, took over the shop and after a year or so married Jacob's mother.

Jacob finished high school and, in spite of his janitorial duties and several other part-time jobs, attended the city campus of the state university, graduating at the age of twenty-one with a degree in business. Friendly with many of the janitors in neighboring buildings, Jacob had learned from these older men about the opportunities in real estate and felt that he would have a good chance in that field. He persuaded his wife-to-be, a niece of his mother's second husband, to study with him for the real estate license examination. When they passed it, they married, and he joined an agency that dealt with industrial properties, while she got a job with a developer of tract housing. He came to be very successful in his line of work. After a few years, his wife was able to quit her job and devote herself to their home and children, as she preferred to do. "You have a lot to be proud of," I said.

SESSIONS 2–6

Mr. Cain responded well to the obvious respect I had for his achievement. Behind his off-putting verbiage was a very well meaning but confused man. His was the familiar story of the poor boy who achieves success and delights in being able to give his children a better life than he could ever have imagined, only to find that his background and his manner of thinking make him an alien in the privileged household he has brought into being.

The immediate problem that I saw confronting the patient, given his wish for understanding and respect from his family, was in the attachment sector of development, where he functioned incompetently. That I had no trouble understanding and validating his genuine achievement served to take the pressure off sufficiently to let me discuss with him how his behavior looked when viewed through the eyes of his children.

As I have illustrated in earlier cases, I find it very effective to orient a patient by finding analogies in a function in which the patient is expert, to clarify the futility of a patently ineffective approach and let a more productive course suggest itself. People are generally excellent psychologists in their own fields of expertise; though they may not be aware of doing so, they know how to use their knowledge of human nature to achieve their goals. Having learned more about Mr. Cain's work and his way of dealing with his clients, I was able to point out how his success depended not so much on the value of the property he was selling but on his ability to grasp the psychological set of the potential buyer. He never *sold* property; he led clients to the conclusion that they needed what he had to offer. Having validated him and supported his self-esteem, I chose to address the behavioral level of the spiral of development by suggesting that he might very well be able to improve the relationship with his children if he took their respective psychological needs into consideration, as he did his clients'. What they said had to be taken in the context of the developmental challenges they were facing at a given time.

Supported by my understanding and feeling less vulnerable, the patient began to be less quick to impose his opinions on various members of the family. Instead, he would contain himself and then report to me what had happened to upset him at home—the school assignment left undone until Sunday night, the fights over who would help with the dishes, the quarreling in the back seat of the car—and in one way or another I would give him approval for his restraint. In the past he had taken all such misconduct as a personal insult, a challenge to his authority; misbehavior was a sign of disrespect for him.

"I never behaved that way as a child," he said.

"You never had a chance to be a child," I replied. And, I went on to explain, it was precisely because his children did not live in chronic anxiety but simply trusted him to be there to take good care of them that they could afford to grow into their responsibilities slowly and behave in the carefree—and to adults often frustrating—ways of childhood. Strange as it may sound, what he was taking as lack of respect was a testament to what he had achieved, not only economically but psychologically. Here again I first took care to validate his achievement, protecting his fragile sense of self-worth, and then helped him to learn something new about himself. For no matter how accurate one's observations may be, the shame-prone person does not hear what is being said until it is clear that at least for the moment the expected attack will not occur.

As the weeks went by, Mr. Cain reported that the atmosphere in the house was becoming significantly less contentious. The children were becoming more involved with him. He found that if he did not immediately criticize their infractions, his wife stepped in soon enough and, when necessary, disciplined the girls effectively. He was a bit chagrined that they listened to her although they had not responded to his admonitions. The difference, I suggested, was that the children were probably made more anxious and disorganized by his personalizing their upset, while his wife's interventions were more straightforward and registered differently on them. I added that in all likelihood he would find himself more effective in these situations now that his anxiety was under better control.

When things became easier at home, Mr. Cain shifted to talking more about his situation at work. Here too he felt belittled, even though he was probably the leading salesman in the organization. When his company moved into a new building, the office he should have had was assigned to another, less productive person. When he complained, he felt he was given the runaround and laughed at. At my request, Mr. Cain gave me a detailed account of his interchange with the office administrator—describing how, as he said, he "remonstrated without recalcitrance"—and it did sound as if they were playing games with him. It seemed to me that his grandiose, self-important manner of speaking, which was meant to shame and establish his superiority over colleagues with a lesser vocabulary, only led people in the office to get revenge for the airs he assumed by depriving him of his due. At that point, however, I did not convey my impression to him.

Then another problematic situation arose. A special performance bonus for which he was eligible was being withheld, and he was being given various spurious explanations. When I asked him what he was doing about it, he again lapsed into pomposity as he told me how he was attempting to demonstrate to the sales manager that justice was on his side. As I listened, I thought that in spite of all his high-flown language, what he was really doing was avoiding a confrontation. He seemed to be skirting the issue rather than insisting on what was rightfully his. I told him as much and wondered out loud whether his tendency to use rather flowery language at times was an indicator of anxiety. If so, what was bothering him? He became red in the face and sat silently in his chair. I said, "I think I have inadvertently embarrassed you. I am sorry about that, but maybe this is the time to look at whatever it is that's going on." He did not reply, and when our session ended shortly thereafter, he left, obviously still disturbed.

Mr. Cain did not come in for his next scheduled session. I phoned his office and left a message for him to call me, but there was no response for two days. I was prepared to call again if he did not keep the following week's appointment, but then I heard from him. His voice had lost its usual salesman-like heartiness; indeed it was tremulous. "I'd better come and see you," he said, and I made room for him that same day.

SESSION 7

MR. CAIN: (*Sits silently, obviously tense and troubled.*)

THERAPIST: You look very concerned. Is it connected to whatever it was that led you to miss your session?

MR. CAIN: (*Nods.*)

THERAPIST: Take your time, but tell me what's happening as soon as you are able.

MR. CAIN: (*Taking a deep breath*) I don't have a business degree. I never attended college . . . any college. (*Hangs his head and cries for several minutes.*)

THERAPIST: And you're very ashamed of not having gone to college.

MR. CAIN: (*Nods his head.*)

THERAPIST: If you didn't go to college you aren't worth much?

MR. CAIN: (*Almost inaudibly*) When I went to interview for the job [with the real estate agency], I knew they only hired college graduates, so I lied. They never checked up on me . . . and I've been lying ever since. See (*holding out his right hand and showing me the class ring on his finger*), I bought this at a pawnshop. I figured they'd see that and believe me.

THERAPIST: And your wife?

MR. CAIN: She knows about it. At the time, she accepted my explanation—I wanted that job. But I don't know.

THERAPIST: Don't know what?

MR. CAIN: She finished college. Her family thought she was marrying beneath her. Maybe she thinks so too, deep down—or maybe not so deep down.

THERAPIST: Meaning?

MR. CAIN: Maybe she thinks she can push me around in front of the kids. Maybe she'll tell them that their father is a fake.

THERAPIST: Fake?

MR. CAIN: We want all of them to go to college: "Study hard, do your homework, read extra in the summer so you'll get into a good school." What if she tells them I never went? that I never got past high school?

THERAPIST: I suppose you'd tell them why.

MR. CAIN: Why?! Why?! Listen, I was up at four in the morning. Who could afford oil burners? I shoveled coal so that there would be heat and hot water. All day long there would be something. There wasn't a day that I didn't get up scared that I'd get sick and couldn't do the work. Where would the money come from for the little ones? Of course, when Hershel took over the shop and married mother, it was a little better, but none of them could have gone past high school if it wasn't . . .

THERAPIST: If it wasn't . . . ?

MR. CAIN: On the side . . . I couldn't get enough money out of the building . . . I worked for a bookie . . . numbers, football cards, the horses. But I only did that for two, three years. Then I started taking buildings on consignment, rehabbed them, and took a piece when they were sold. That money I put aside for them.

THERAPIST: And your brothers and sister got to go to school?

MR. CAIN: (*Proud and no longer ashamed*) Every one of them. A dentist, a teacher, and a nurse.

THERAPIST: Well, I guess that's what you'll tell them.

MR. CAIN: Tell who?

THERAPIST: Your daughters, if the question of your having gone to college ever comes up. That is a wonderful and touching story— impressive, too.

MR. CAIN: I'm sure they'll want to hear it. We've spoiled them.

THERAPIST: I think they would listen and feel very good about you. It's only when your insecurity gets the better of you and you try to force respect that things go wrong. Don't your brothers and sister appreciate what you did? I would certainly think they would.

MR. CAIN: Oh, sure. But I don't see them much. I talk to them on the phone. But since my girls got older, we don't visit back and forth.

THERAPIST: On account of . . . ?

MR. CAIN: On account of what if they start talking in front of the kids about school and things . . .

THERAPIST: You're afraid that your secret will be betrayed. That their aunt and uncles might drop the awful truth that their father is a self-made man to whom they owe everything they have.

MR. CAIN: If you put it *that* way . . .

THERAPIST: That's the way everyone, except you, would put it. Don't your brothers and sister let you know that?

MR. CAIN: They think of me like a second father, which I was. They want to get together, but I put them off. They probably think I'm a little crazy. I guess I am.

THERAPIST: Not crazy, but ashamed. False shame, in your case. Shame that is destroying everything you could and should have. As if a college degree were the passport to respectability.

MR. CAIN: It's easy for you to say that; you went.

THERAPIST: And I know exactly what it can and cannot do for you. That is why everyone with a college degree will admire you for having accomplished what you did without the preparation that college can give. But I'm not trying to minimize your feelings. What *is* important is that you do feel inferior to others, that you feel you have a defect that you must conceal. Anyhow, where did you develop your vocabulary?

MR. CAIN: What do you mean?

THERAPIST: You know, those long words you tend to use, especially when you get nervous. It sounds to me as if, like your class ring, it's something you acquired in the belief that people would take you for a college graduate.

MR. CAIN: (*Visibly embarrassed once again*) One of the tenants in the building, when they moved—I don't know where or how they got it—threw out a brand-new Webster's Unabridged; the cellophane was still on it. I took it. Every morning I tried to learn five new words and their synonyms; then, during the day, I would practice using them in my head as I went about my janitorial obligations. You think it was a dumb idea, I suppose. I know . . . they make fun of me at the office.

THERAPIST: It was your way of getting an education, and it wasn't a bad idea. It becomes a problem when you use your vocabulary to try to mask your shame. Then it comes across as affected. It's the shame that's the problem.

MR. CAIN: I guess you're right, but even so, that's the way I feel. You can't make it go away, can you? Neither can I.

THERAPIST: Not abracadabra, but here we are, you and I, talking together about something that, until now, was a terrible secret. So we'll see where it goes. However, what I'm wondering about is how much your shame is going to cost you this week.

MR. CAIN: Cost? How?

THERAPIST: The bonus that you're afraid to ask for—how much is it supposed to be?

MR. CAIN: Twenty-four.

THERAPIST: Twenty-four?

MR. CAIN: Twenty-four thousand.

THERAPIST: Wow!

MR. CAIN: That's what it comes to. It was a contest, and I won it. I've been number one for three years straight.

THERAPIST: And now they're reneging?

MR. CAIN: Seems that way, doesn't it?

THERAPIST: What recourse do you have?

MR. CAIN: Go to the president, I guess. He'll have to give it to me—it's in writing.

THERAPIST: But you haven't talked to him?

MR. CAIN: No, just the sales manager. He's the one playing games.

THERAPIST: Maybe you're letting him, because you feel vulnerable. Maybe you feel that, not having gone to college, you're not entitled to earn this kind of money. You can't hold your head up and ask for what's yours.

MR. CAIN: They don't like me. They have to keep me, I'm a big earner. But they think I'm different from them.

THERAPIST: You are.

MR. CAIN: What?!

THERAPIST: They can't figure you out. When you speak in that stilted manner you have, it makes them uncomfortable. They get anxious and then attack you.

MR. CAIN: What should I do?

THERAPIST: You sold the properties, didn't you?

MR. CAIN: I certainly did.

THERAPIST: Well, let's see what happens—or, rather, what you make happen.

Mr. Cain's life was dominated by a pervasive sense of shame. The "attack other" defense that he used with his family, the "withdrawal" defense that he showed when he shied away from confronting his sales manager, and the "avoidance" defense manifested in his pretentious language were all secondary to the "attack self" mode that governed his life. As I learned, he despised himself for not being a college graduate. He believed it marked him as inferior, and he anticipated being humiliated by anyone who came to know his secret. Of course, I learned about this only later; what confronted me initially was a person using verbosity to convince me of his significance, when in fact his accomplishments were all the recommendation he needed. His achievements were made all the more impressive by his background, which one would think would have militated against success.

The disorganizing effect of shame cannot be overestimated. Mr. Cain had to be very intelligent and clever to have gotten where he was, but his intelligence did not help him in matters where he felt vulnerable to humiliation. Though initially he presented himself as someone with difficulties in the attachment sector of development—his problem with his family—these difficulties were secondary to failure in the autonomy sector. He could not realize himself as an individual. Not respecting himself, he believed that no one who came to know him would take him seriously, either. When I oriented myself through the developmental spiral, his history in the area of autonomy or independent functioning, as he told it to me, showed no problem with decision making, behavioral implementation, or the attainment of competence. It was the reward, the self-esteem that one would expect to follow such a sequence, that eluded him. His pompous speech was clearly defensive, but to have confronted him early on with its absurdity and the futility of using it to engender respect would have been not only cruel but ineffective. Mr. Cain's prolixity indicated the degree of anxiety that threatened him. Initially, confronting his verbosity would have led him either to flee from treatment, to ignore what he heard, or to redouble his defensive mannerisms.

Until one can offer such patients a viable substitute, they have no choice but to continue to ward off anxiety in the only way they know how.

This last point was nicely illustrated in Mr. Cain's situation. Although his wife had repeatedly objected to his overbearing attempts to assert authority, her complaints only led him to try even harder to impose his ideas on the family until, in desperation, she threatened divorce. It was the anxiety created by that threat that pulled him up short and brought him, albeit reluctantly, to search for a more viable alternative to his accustomed behavior. Common sense would dictate that he should simply have examined his priorities and altered his behavior accordingly, but that is not how people operate when the cohesion and vitality of the self feels threatened. Most of the problems that patients bring to us admit of a fairly straightforward solution, but, as we know, the good advice we could give would fall on deaf ears. To put it operationally, advice offered too early would not mitigate the anxiety sufficiently to give the patient the freedom to try out a new solution. Yet later, if treatment is successful, our suggestions do become effective. Why the change?

Shame is the affect that makes us feel all alone. This feeling is illustrated dramatically in the example of Baby Alan's reaction to his mother's disapproval. The baby's eyes search the mother's face for the expected welcoming response but do not find it. Her eyes are not wide with joy; they are narrowed, and her brow is furrowed. Her mouth is tight, not widened by a smile. Alan, overwhelmed by this interruption of his positive expectation, breaks eye contact and hangs his head. Since his nascent sense of self is very much dependent on his mother's validating expression and body language, his psychological viability is truly endangered. This unbearable lostness is what at a later age shame threatens to revive. The intensity of the shame reaction to the mother's reproof may make no sense from an adult perspective, but the emergency measures instituted to prevent a recurrence of this catastrophic response to being shamed are perfectly understandable when the source and enormity of the threat are understood.

It is relatively easy to restore psychological balance in the early years by showing the child that contact has not been withdrawn permanently, that the child's basic worth is not being questioned. In later life, when someone like Jacob Cain has taken his worthlessness as a given and now seeks only to minimize the attendant pain of that belief, the problem becomes compounded. A vicious circle has been created. He needs the reassuring contact of a supportive figure to begin to feel whole, but letting his need be seen requires revealing the reason for it. Since he is convinced that such a revelation must inevitably generate shame, he cannot afford to open himself up. And so, paradoxically but understandably, his isolation grows as his need grows.

Mr. Cain's case underscores again the necessity of not simply focusing on a patient's problems or the incompetencies that give rise to them but of taking stock of the psychological assets as well. As I have emphasized repeatedly, it is the latter that give one a place on which to stand and get leverage on the former. The patient's assets not only show what the therapist has to work with but open the window of opportunity for offsetting the paralyzing sense of shame.

As I reviewed Mr. Cain's first session, it became clear that his mismanagement of his relations with his wife and children was not at the core of the difficulty. To have focused on this and questioned the justification or efficacy of his behavior would only have led to further rationalization of his view of these transactions and probably would have set up an adversarial relationship between us. I would have been seen as functioning as his wife's agent, delegated to whip him into shape. That, of course, had to be avoided, so as soon as he gave me an opportunity, I segued into another aspect of his life. When he mentioned that he would never have treated his father with the disdain his children showed him, I asked him to tell me about that relationship. Deprived as his early life was, his straightforward manner of talking about these years indicated to me that in itself his family's poverty was not the source of his shame—the shame that I assumed had led him to his wordiness and to his failed search for respect from his children.

Without even knowing the particulars of his sense of humiliation, it seemed right to me to underscore what he had been able to accomplish: "You have a lot to be proud of." I did not say that simply because he deserved it, or because I wanted to make him feel good, or because I was trying to show him that I was a nice guy. A patient preoccupied with defending himself against a threat that dominates his life does not have enough psychological flexibility left over for the work of psychotherapy. My purpose was to begin to build, plank by plank, the floor of deserved self-respect that he needed to support him as we moved forward. It was my way of beginning to establish contact with this man who, in ways that had yet to be discovered, had been so traumatized by shame that his genuinely competent achievements did not give him the self-esteem to which he was entitled.

On the basis of present-day knowledge of normal development, it was possible to anticipate in principle the issues Mr. Cain was facing and to intervene accordingly. By implication, I said to Mr. Cain that, though I had no idea what he had done to bring such shame on himself, it sounded to me that what he had accomplished deserved to be recognized and admired. It was only later that my respect for him permitted him to reveal the truth of his situation.

When validation is successful, patients' anticipation that they will be shamed—that their defects will be seen to count much more than either their assets or their good intentions—diminishes sufficiently to let them hear the therapist's interventions as well meant rather than humiliating. Indeed, the question of whether short-term therapy can be effective or whether lengthier treatment is needed often depends not so much on the nature of the problem per se but on how soon patients can permit themselves to feel safe, supported, and enhanced in the therapeutic relationship. The more that therapists are aware of the nature and development of affect and its central role in mental life, the more likely they are to be able to identify a patient's needs accurately and respond to them appropriately.

I took Mr. Cain's reports that his irascibility with his family was becoming less of a problem as evidence that my ability to validate what he had accomplished was ameliorating his sensitivity to real or imagined slights and letting him cope better with his family. If that had been the main issue, he might very well have told me that his need for therapy had come to an end. What happened instead, not unexpectedly, was that he ventured to talk about an aspect of his life that was even more humiliating—namely, his inability to get the respect of his colleagues in spite of his superior performance.

I thought I understood why he was not given the office space he should have had when his group moved to new quarters. Not only was his high-flown language resented, but the insecurity behind it probably signaled itself to his peers as it had to me. I imagined that the people in his office sensed that he could not and would not stand up for himself in a straightforward manner. Whether they thwarted him just to make sport or whether he was cheated of his space in order to do a favor for someone else is something I did not try to find out. Indeed, I did not say much of anything. Unlike the situation with his wife and children, which was ongoing and could potentially be altered, here the damage was done and probably could not be reversed. It was enough that he had been able to tell me of his humiliation, and I felt that at this point it would only reinforce his sense of worthlessness if I engaged him in a discussion about what he might have done and why he did not do it.

The bonus that was being dangled in front of him without being delivered, however, was another matter. What he did or did not do still could make a difference. Because I had established myself as someone who understood him and could be trusted to value him, I felt safe in confronting him. Here, once again, was that crucial juncture where patients, presenting themselves as victims, are shown that they are the agents of their downfall. In Mr. Cain's case, his conviction of worthlessness and the anticipation of being refused and further shamed if he dared assert himself were leading him to behave in self-destructive ways. There was no question that he was being treated cavalierly. The world would be a better place if one did not often have to struggle to get what one has already earned, but that is beside the point.

Inevitably such a confrontation is itself an occasion for shame for those prone to it, but, like the mother who shows that she values the child even though she disapproves of the behavior, I could face Mr. Cain with the fact that in this instance I did not accept what he was doing. Furthermore, I anticipated that his wish for my approval would serve as an incentive to bite the bullet and do what he had to do, not only to get his money but to save his self-respect. And that is what happened. He found himself able to be assertive, and as soon as he ceased to be evasive, he received what he was owed. He was not only pleased with himself and proud of what he had done but able to be quite objective about his behavior before and after our crucial session. As is usually the case, once patients find a viable alternative that lets them escape the vicious circle in which they are caught, they can look much more objectively on how they have inadvertently undermined themselves in the past.

I now tried to have Mr. Cain consider why it was that the absence of a college degree had proved to be so crucial for his sense of self over the years. What he became aware of was his anger that even in a neighborhood of poor people he had been relatively worse off than his peers. For years he had managed to hide this resentment even from himself, maintaining, as he originally told me, that he simply accepted the hand that was dealt him. Boxed in by his mother's helplessness and his father's emotional handicaps, he had felt that he had no choice but to accept the role in which his parents cast him. Even as other families around him made the sacrifices that let their children get a higher education, he did not let himself become bitter but instead, and as if it were his fault, became increasingly ashamed that he had not gone further than high school. He isolated himself from his former friends and acted as if it were they who were shunning him. And, though his determination that his siblings would not be left behind bore fruit, the compromises he had to make to achieve their security left him vulnerable to a sense of inferiority that he then felt he had to overcome. It was helpful to him to realize that he could afford to become aware of the anger he harbored as it related to his lost childhood without thereby rejecting or ceasing to love his parents.

Mr. Cain was doing well. In his sessions with me and, it seemed, at home and in the office, he was not trying so hard to produce an impression of erudition. Confident of his worth, he did not take umbrage so quickly or search out imagined slights. He felt sufficiently at ease to invite his siblings and their families to his home once again. I was content with his progress but not satisfied that I really understood why he suffered so much from the lack of a college degree. Why should anger that others had opportunities lost to him turn into shame, especially since he had more than compensated for the absence of a higher education? In my mind, the lie he had told years ago to get a start in real estate was not a sufficient explanation for his self-doubt. After all, it was not the only time he had cut corners when he felt he had to do so to get a foothold on the next rung of the ladder, and, though he was not proud of the compromises he had made, they did not devastate him. Even in psychoanalysis, however, with all the opportunities for in-depth exploration of a patient's mental life, the roots of pathology are by no means invariably uncovered. I therefore resigned myself to not knowing and focused on helping Mr. Cain consolidate his gains. In the twelfth session, we reviewed the course of the therapy and decided that we would end treatment after giving ourselves two more meetings in which to see if there were any loose ends that needed to be tied up.

Having decided to end, Mr. Cain was at a loss as to what to do with the remainder of our session. "Let's just go on as we always do," I said. His thoughts turned to a cookout at his sister's house to which they had been invited. Her children were musical, and while he was glad for their talent, he knew he would be expected to sit and listen to them perform, and that bored him. Then came some thoughts about children being spoiled for life's challenges if too much of a fuss is made over them. He felt his wife had a tendency to be too involved with the comings and goings of their daughters. No one had paid much attention to him when he was a kid. As he said in a familiar refrain, "There was work to do."

He then recalled a scene from his childhood that he had not thought about in years but that he remembered clearly. The women of the neighborhood would come to his father's shop to have their husbands' good clothes altered, mended, or pressed. And since no man owned more than one or two pairs of pants, certainly never more than one suit, the women would sit and wait for the work to be done so that the clothes could be worn again the next day. Sometimes there would be quite an assembly, and, as voices rose, the conversation always became a proud and competitive recital of the achievements of the various speakers' children. Living as he did behind the store, as far back as he can remember he heard how this one's son played the violin like Heifetz and that one's daughter got all A's on her report card. And of course, as he got older, so did the children of his father's customers, and the talk would be of who had gotten scholarships and what professions they aspired to. When he was in the store, the mothers would ask him what his ambitions were. His stock answer always was a short "I gotta work now."

This pocket of memories opened up a new area of inquiry for us. It turned out that what was crucial was not so much the anger that others, though also poor, had opportunities that were denied him, as we had discussed, but the proud tones in which the mothers sang their children's praises. He only now understood how desperately he had wanted to hear something like that from his parents. During his childhood, no one ever told him that what he was doing was appreciated. The emphasis was always on what could happen if he did not fulfill his obligations; "Do good and behave yourself—your father's got enough troubles" was his mother's parting admonition most mornings as he left for school. But when he did well, there was no acknowledgment of his achievement, nor was there praise for essentially taking his father's place when any heavy work had to be done.

Mr. Cain could now contrast my effortless praise and admiration for his accomplishments with the absence of that kind of appreciation in his formative years. In retrospect, we agreed that my suggestion in the first session that he had much to be proud of had opened the way for his later "confession" and all that followed.

Under the circumstances, we agreed to forget the termination date to see where these insights would lead. Actually, it did not take too long to complete our work. It seemed to us that, as children under stress often do, Jacob (unlike Mr. Dale), instead of importuning his parents to acknowledge him, blamed himself and became ashamed. The grateful acknowledgment he eventually received from his siblings, whose future he had assured, did not compensate for or address the initial trauma. His attempts to impose his will and his opinions on his wife and children, which had initially brought him to therapy, could be seen as his way of trying to get their approbation without having to admit to himself or his family how much he needed it.

We spent some time discussing the fact that his daughters should be assumed to have needs similar to those he had as a youngster and reexamining his relationship with them. He recognized that in his preoccupation with himself he had not given them enough credit where credit was due. In the process of correcting this situation, he found himself enjoying his fatherhood much more than he ever had.

In our eighteenth session, the therapy was concluded by mutual agreement. We met again in six months and then a year later to monitor his situation, and I found that he had maintained his improvement. He had thought briefly about going to college on a part-time basis to earn the degree the lack of which had bothered him so terribly, but he had decided against it. When he was asked to give some lectures on real estate as a career at a local junior college, he felt pleased and proud to do so. He correctly took it as all the more complimentary that he, who lacked a formal higher education, should be asked to serve as a teacher.

USING THE PATIENT'S STRENGTH
TO BUILD SELF-ESTEEM

Mr. Cain provides us with a convincing demonstration of the over-riding significance of psychic reality. His solid accomplishments could not offset the inner sense of worthlessness that first shamed him and then led to the defensive maneuvers that were making him a laughingstock at the office and a problem at home. The sad but ludicrous nature of this shame-prone man's attempted compensation highlights an issue that is seen frequently in psychotherapeutic practice but usually not so blatantly.

Mr. Cain's very important recollections about the lack of recognition and acknowledgment for his contribution to the family, which seemed to clarify the specific dynamics that led to his painful attempts at achieving competence, did not become apparent until we had almost concluded his treatment. His shame, however, poorly concealed by attempts at erudition, was an unmistakable signpost of a problem that needed to be addressed before any significant progress could be made in his treatment. Mr. Cain's attempt to impress and win admiration by posing as a walking dictionary announced to me his need for validation of his worth. Implicitly he signaled the goal he sought but could not reach. Becoming acquainted with his life and his achievements made it possible for me to extend to him the validation he needed to soothe his shame, at least for the moment. I expressed my appreciation for what he had accomplished before I understood anything of what had shamed him so. The immediate effect of this intervention was to make it less necessary for him to try to force his family's acknowledgment. His change in behavior opened the way to competence in his relationships at home and laid the groundwork for further exploratory work.

Rather than dealing only with the behavior that had precipitated his coming to see me—the manner in which he was dealing with his wife and children—I worked with what my developmental diagram told me were the reasons for his behavior. Once I had decided that the discrepancy that gave rise to pathology lay between his considerable strengths and his unnecessarily low self-esteem, that became the issue on which I focused my efforts. That is, I initiated a treatment aimed at uncovering and correcting the etiology of the problem rather than at the symptoms the problem generated. This is, of course, the goal of all therapy, be it surgical, pharmacological, or psychological. If one understands and can do something about the etiology of the problem, then the self-defeating behavior, no longer necessary, will be eliminated.

Confronting such patients initially with the counterproductive nature of their attitude and behavior is useless. One might as well point out to a man on crutches that these are but poor substitutes for his legs. Until such a patient's injury has healed and the limb has been restored to function, the crutches are needed lest he collapse in a heap. Patients will not and cannot relinquish their self-protective measures until they can believe and trust in a more reliable way of accommodating themselves. Just as a broken leg must be splinted so it can heal, so a spirit broken by shame needs the support that a therapist can give until vulnerability has been replaced by sound adaptational measures.

Therapists often fear that positive statements of the sort I made in this case will let patients use such validation to seal over their problems. And indeed in the treatment of psychoneurotic patients in traditional psychoanalysis such comments can short-circuit the transference and prevent conflicted material from coming into the therapy. As the experience with Mr. Cain illustrates, however, in many situations, being acknowledged by the therapist as more than a bundle of pathology often provides that necessary substitute for the defensive crutch upon which the patient has had to lean. By hanging on to the therapist's arm, the patient can practice walking without the crutch until further work allows the person to proceed unaided.

But what if one's attempt to validate a patient fails to accomplish anything, and nothing seems to happen? No harm is done. As always, one reevaluates the developmental issues and goes on from there. More often than not, the failure of one's attempts at buttressing a patient's deserved self-esteem is an indication that the capacity to rely on the therapist is not in place. In other words, if the patient does not have the expectation that the therapist is willing and able to help, the therapist does not have the power to be effective in other than superficial ways.

Many patients clearly signal that they are looking for a quasi-parental authority on whom they can rely. For example, Mrs. Willingham's comment that she came to see me because of her previous positive experience with psychoanalysis was a good indicator of her readiness to trust me to be of help to her. But apart from such declarations, the best indicator that a positive transference is in place is an ambience in the therapeutic relationship akin to that of a good pupil/teacher or child/parent relationship. It is one in which each partner feels comfortable in his or her role.

CHAPTER 6

Validating a Change:
Franklin Furlong

PARADOXICAL AS IT MAY SEEM, there are patients who come
for therapy because of anxiety related to a positive character
change that has been generated by the interplay of experience
and life's circumstances. Although their new sense of self is most welcome, it has come into conflict with previously established and still
viable ways for maintaining self-esteem. Here the therapeutic challenge is to help the patient identify the nature of that conflict so that
it may be dealt with appropriately.

FRANKLIN FURLONG

There was something familiar about his voice when he called to make
an appointment, but I did not place it until Dr. Franklin Furlong was
actually in my office. He had been one of a group of family practice
physicians and internists to whom I had given a series of lectures on
psychotherapy some four or five years previously. Dr. Furlong was a
well-dressed man whose athletic build and craggy features made him
appear much younger than his sixty years. He had come, he said,

because "I need to talk to someone about whether or not I need to talk to someone."

DR. FURLONG: You're going to think I'm crazy—not a good thing to say to a psychiatrist—I mean, you're not going to believe this.

THERAPIST: Well, let's see. Go right ahead.

DR. FURLONG: This all started about six months ago, on a Friday night. I had to go to a meeting; my wife had one, too. Since we didn't want to take both cars downtown, we'd agreed she'd pick me up later that night. That meant I had to get a cab when I finished at the office; it would have taken too long to walk.

THERAPIST: Okay.

DR. FURLONG: Since I usually drive, I had forgotten that this was going to be a big deal at 5:30 in the afternoon. It turned out that everybody else was also wanting taxis. Every cab was full. After a while, I started walking, figuring I'd pick up a cab somewhere along the way. Sure enough, after a couple of blocks, I spotted an office building where there were cabs with their signs lit, and I headed up that way. Of course, by the time I got there they had all been taken, but I figured it was as good a place as any to stop and wait. And a few minutes later I did see an empty cab approaching. I stepped into the street and raised my arm to hail it. At that moment a young woman appeared at my side and, with a hint of irritation in her voice, said something to me; the only words I caught were "in line."

"Oh," I asked apologetically, "have I jumped the line? Are people in line for taxis?"

"No," she said, and added quite firmly, "but I was here first." I guess she must have been waiting farther up the street. She had apparently seen me, but I had not seen her.

I was about to be big about it and offer her the cab, when something made me ask in which direction she was going.

"North," she said.

"So am I."

We quickly established that it would make sense to share the ride. The cab would drop me off first and take her a few blocks farther to her destination. By then the cab had pulled up, and we got in. She slid all the way over on the seat against the left-hand door, and I, taking the hint, stayed in the right-hand corner. The large purse that had been slung over her shoulder—looked expensive, probably a Coach—sat between us. So, decorously settled, we looked and really saw each other for the first time across the expanse that separated us.

I don't know what she saw, but . . . Do you like opera?

THERAPIST: Some.

DR. FURLONG: *Don Pasquale?*

THERAPIST: Love it. In spite of the fact that my musically correct friends tell me that I shouldn't. I hear it at every opportunity.

DR. FURLONG: Me too. Anyway, then you know the gasp of astonishment and delight that Don Pasquale gives when Norina, in the guise of Sofronia Malatesta, raises her veil?

THERAPIST: Indeed I do.

DR. FURLONG: That's the experience I had. This was a beautiful woman. She had a most attractive face: no makeup, a little overbite—something that always gets me—blondish hair that hung straight to the collar of her coat and framed her face just right. That fresh, young face could have been on a magazine cover. I even wondered momentarily whether she was a fashion model. Not tall enough, I thought, though what was visible of her legs looked very pretty, too. I checked her hand—no wedding or engagement ring.

"Do you work in that building?" I asked her, and volunteered that I had walked over from my office in search of transportation, indirectly also letting her know that my unfamiliarity with her immediate environment excused me from whatever faux pas I had committed in trying to appropriate our now-shared taxi.

"Yes," she said, "I do. And I'm sure glad it's Friday."

"Oh? What kind of work are you in?"

"I'm an attorney," she said, flashing me a smile that I interpreted as either apologetic or indicating that she was still very new to her profession and not yet secure in her title.

"What sort of law do you practice?"

"My firm does mainly debtor/creditor reorganization and business restructuring. That's fancy for 'bankruptcy.' And you?"

"I'm a physician, a heart specialist—a cardiologist."

"I guess that's not so easy, either."

"Right, it's hard work, but often very gratifying. There are wonderful things we can do now for people."

There was a pause in our conversation, and thoughts that had provided a background for our chitchat now moved to the forefront of my mind. Fate had thrown me into the company of probably the most attractive woman I'd conversed with in years. Obviously intelligent, at ease with herself, charming and friendly. Where were you thirty years ago, even ten years ago? Speaking of Don Pasquale, here I was, an old man lusting after a woman probably not much older than my kids. I pictured myself trying to become more familiar, asking her name, and she indignantly refusing to give it. Or offering her my card, only to have her talk about it later to her lover, both of them having a good laugh at the old fool making a pass. Better take the high road.

She broke the silence, which in a few seconds more would have become awkward, smiling and asking—was she reading my thoughts?—"How long have you been practicing?"

I smiled in return, rather benignly, I thought. "More than thirty years—longer, I think, than you've been on this earth."

"Mmm, I guess that's right—twenty-eight."

Well, that settles that for sure, I thought. If it hadn't been obvious before, the enormity of the gap in our ages was only too apparent to her now. "You can't be a partner yet? How many years before your class comes up?"

"You know about law firms."

"Sure, many of my friends—and patients, too—are attorneys."

"Well, you're right, I've got a few years to go—if I stay in bankruptcy."

"You might switch?"

"I'm not sure."

I don't dare ask her about marriage plans. She'll realize I'm angling to see if she's available. No sense asking when I'm only going to be humiliated.

"Traffic is pretty bad tonight, isn't it?" says she.

"Yes, yes, indeed it is," I agree. For once I'm grateful to be in a traffic jam, but we are nevertheless inching closer to the corner where I get off.

"You're going to visit friends here, Doctor?"

"No, I have a meeting to go to tonight."

"On Friday night?"

"No rest for the wicked."

How original! Now, in the movies Maurice Chevalier would say, "You are so right. What I would really like to do is to take a beautiful young woman dancing; would you care to make my dream come true?" He got away with it till the day he died. What a coward I am—almost at my corner—serves me right.

She is fumbling with her purse, obviously ready to begin negotiating how we will split the fare. I fish for my wallet, take out a five and a couple of singles, enough to cover the meter and a decent tip. "Here we go," I say, dropping the bills in her now open purse. I think she is a little surprised that there is no attempt on my part to figure out what "my half" comes to. Such a nice old man; such a generous daddy.

"Right here, please." Open the door. One last smile: "Goodbye, Counselor . . . pleasure to have met you . . . have a good weekend."

"It was nice . . . thanks for sharing . . . enjoy your meeting."

I didn't pay much attention to the proceedings that evening; I kept reliving that interlude. Driving home, after my wife called for me, I was mostly silent. But that's not anything unusual. We don't talk much unless there is a problem with the kids or the house. I thought I'd have trouble falling asleep that night, but I didn't. I slept well.

Saturday I had to go to the office, and as I got ready to go, filling my pockets with the usual stuff, I realized that my wallet wasn't there. A search of the suit I'd worn didn't turn up anything. I looked on the floor; I retraced my steps to the front door and then into the garage—nothing. One last possibility: In the downstairs closet I checked the raincoat I'd had on, and in it, to my puzzlement, I did find some bills, but no wallet. It was really gone, not just misplaced. It surprised me that it didn't seem to bother me that much. Of course, I don't carry any big sums of money, so that was no big loss. And I belong to one of those outfits where a call cancels all your credit cards; I got that done. I must have a dozen wallets lying around from Christmases and birthdays. I grabbed one of them, got a few dollars more from my wife's purse, and took off.

Driving down, I realized that my Friday encounter was still with me. Once I got to the office, I made a resolution to get busy and put that taxi ride out of my mind before the inner glow gave way to anger and bitterness—what could have been/should have been—I know those feelings too well.

Sunday I had my usual headache, read the papers, and caught up on some stuff around the house.

Monday I ran over to the driver's license bureau and got a replacement. The day was a long one, and there was no time to think about anything but work, even if I'd wanted to. It was after five when my secretary buzzed me and said someone had come with my wallet. Then it hit me: the last time I had it in my hand was in the cab. Damn, the driver picked it up and, instead of turning it in to the lost-and-found and having me notified, held out so he himself could bring it to my office and collect a reward.

"Okay, send him in," I called into the intercom. I was doubly irritated: I'd been put to unnecessary trouble by his dilatory behavior, and now I'd have to give him a tip to boot. For some reason the phrase "A day late and a dollar short" ran through my mind.

Doctor, when she walked in, I had an experience I've only read about: I swear, in that moment of recognition my whole life flashed before me. I should be speechless, I remember thinking. Instead I heard myself say, without hesitating or stammering and in a heartfelt tone that didn't sound at all like me, "Thank God you've come." We drew closer, embraced, kissed—not passionately, not lengthily, but not perfunctorily, either. Two people acknowledging that they belong together.

"What do we do now?"

"We go to dinner. Since you know my name and I don't know yours, and I still don't have my wallet, I get to choose the restaurant."

I'm different, Doctor. From the moment my little attorney walked into my life—you see, I'm still afraid to say her name out loud, as if it will all turn out to be only a dream—I've become someone I don't recognize. I know that I'm seen as a dour, distant, even arrogant sort of fellow. Never say much. Reliable, know my stuff—good, but not warm. I've made no effort to reach out, to be friendly. I've lost patients because of my personality; I know that. All of a sudden I *was* Maurice Chevalier—attractive, charming, full of life; my years only make me more desirable. I'm watching myself saying all the right things and haven't a clue as to where they are coming from. Today I am that person that—somewhere in my head, I guess—I've always fantasied I could be. . . . I can tell you something I wouldn't say to anyone else: I love her very much, but, at long last, I love me, too.

THERAPIST: Quite a story.

DR. FURLONG: It's not over yet. Here's the part you'll like.

We—that is, Elise and I—(*Smiles*) I guess it's safe—Elise Banting—are seated in a really nice place I know. In a booth, quiet, and very private. We order wine. Neither one of us is doing much talking, mostly just looking at each other like two moonstruck kids. I think, I'd better say something. "I've never been so happy about losing a wallet. As a matter of fact, that was a first. I've never lost a wallet before, or, for that matter, anything important. I can't imagine how it happened. Did you find it on the floor after I left?"

"No, my love, you didn't lose it."

That "love" doubled—at least doubled—my heart rate. There's a tightening in my chest. Great, all I need right now is a coronary.

"I didn't lose it?"

"You reached for your wallet, opened it, took out some money, put it in your pocket, leaned over, and dropped your wallet into my purse."

"A real Freudian slip, by God."

"Me too. I knew later that I'd seen you do exactly what you did, but it didn't register. When the cab got to my house—my mind was so much on you, I guess . . . " (*Keep your left hand in your lap, your right one on the table. Under no circumstances will you check your pulse.*) ". . . that without thinking about it I reached in my purse, paid off the driver, and went upstairs. It wasn't till Monday morning, when I switched purses, that your wallet tumbled out, and the whole scene came back. Then, of course, I realized that what had hit me in those few minutes we rode together was mutual; after that it was easy."

"I can't tell you how grateful I am."

At that moment the wine was served. We raised our glasses and, as if with one voice, gave our first toast: "To Freud."

Here Dr. Furlong paused and looked at me expectantly. What to say? So far I had learned a good deal about his strengths: he was an accomplished, effectively functioning professional, he was acquainted with his emotions and capable of thinking about them, and he had excellent narrative skills. As yet, however, I did not know why he was here. The sectors of autonomy, affect and reason, and creativity seem to be in good order. I had not heard about psychosexuality, but the odds are high that a problem in that area would by now have been woven into the narrative by this voluble, straightforward man. In the sector of attachment, it was clear that his marriage was far from fulfilling for him, but if Elise was the solution, where did I come in?

In terms of the positive transference, I saw no immediate issues. He had heard me speak some years previously, and that encounter had apparently created a sufficiently positive connection to let him turn to me now. His open way of speaking about the events that had changed his life underscored a sense of kinship and a willingness to rely on me. He had reached for affirmation of that kinship when he involved me in an exchange about Donizetti's opera. I could simply have replied in the affirmative when he asked if I was familiar with *Don Pasquale*, but the buoyancy with which he asked his question would have made a simple "yes" deflating, and so I chose to reach out to him with a personal comment. Either that would strengthen the bond we were forging, or, if he shrank from that familiarity or became disdainful of my taste, it would tell me something about how he viewed our relationship. If I had not been familiar with the piece, I would not just have said "no" but, in the interest of strengthening kinship, would have said something like, "No, if I have heard it, I can't say I remember much about it. Why don't you paint the background for the comparison you are about to make." The expression of my interest would have served as a substitute for the bond he hoped was already there. A little later, his overcoming his superstitious hesitation and telling me the name of his beloved underscored his readiness to rely on my skill to help him. But, again, help him with what? My immediate task was to orient myself and him to whatever issues if any might be there to be dealt with psychotherapeutically.

THERAPIST: You sound very animated and happy, but we still have to answer your initial question as to whether or not you need to speak with a psychotherapist. Something brought you here, and that is what we need to clarify.

DR. FURLONG: Hmmm, I thought it might become obvious to you. Something is making me anxious, I guess, but I don't know what.

I am happy as never before, but there is a sort of underlying discomfort whose source I can't identify.

THERAPIST: What is your situation now vis-à-vis your wife and Elise?

DR. FURLONG: I see Elise every day, and we have gone away on weekends when that was possible. We had a week together in California when I went to a convention. I can tell you, I didn't go to many of the sessions, and it was wonderful. I would like nothing better than to move out and live with her, but my lawyer told me not to leave until we had a property settlement.

THERAPIST: So you have discussed divorce with your wife?

DR. FURLONG: Yes, within weeks of our getting together. Let me go back. I went with Elise to her place after that first dinner, and we just kept on talking and talking. Each kept telling the other that we had to be careful and not do anything rash, but the more we talked the clearer it became that we had found what we each were looking for. Although we necked around like a couple of high school kids, we both understood without saying so that what was between us was too serious to be resolved by getting into bed. I finally left around four in the morning, walking on air and not the least bit tired.

THERAPIST: And your wife? What did she say when you came in?

DR. FURLONG: I don't know if she heard me come in. We've had separate bedrooms for years. There have been plenty of nights that I haven't come home at all. She sleeps late in the morning; she chooses to believe I left early if I'm not there. She's good at deluding herself when she needs to. I keep a fresh suit, shirt, and stuff at my club for such occasions.

THERAPIST: But you brought up divorce?

DR. FURLONG: Oh, sure. But not right away. Elise and I continued to get together, of course. We tried to be grown up and realistic. I confronted her with the obvious: thirty-two years. If she wanted children, I might well not be there to help her raise them to maturity. Even without kids, under the best of circumstances she'll end up a middle-aged widow who spent her youth on an old man. And what if old age does me in? She'll be playing nurse to an invalid while she's in her prime. That she doesn't need.

Elise would say that I'm younger and in better shape than men half my age she's been with—there was a boyfriend who didn't last a week after we met—and besides, children were not a priority for her. It turns out she had her tubes tied a few years before; like mine, her childhood was no picnic, and motherhood did not appeal to her. She'd argue that there was no guarantee that she would outlive me, and if she got sick, would I not want to nurse her? Of course, I had to answer in the affirmative.

She would argue that maybe I should not marry her, because she was too inexperienced and uninteresting for a man of my supposed erudition. Actually, as I told her, she was wise beyond her years, and I found her totally absorbing. What about the money? she'd want to know. As an attorney, even though not specializing in matrimonial law, she was well aware of the financial implications of divorce and how a man in a hurry to remarry could be taken to the cleaners by an indignant wife and a sharp, determined lawyer. I countered with the fact that my wife has inherited wealth. She is much richer than I am. But, Doctor, I always insisted—after the few years it took to get my practice off the ground—that we have separate accounts and live on my income alone. Anyway, as I told Elise, I have accumulated enough that if a court were to give her half of everything that's mine and even force me into some kind of additional settlement, it would not affect my life-style. When all you have is work, it's amazing how fast the money piles up.

So we went back and forth, trying to talk the other out of what we each wanted more than anything. After a while it'd be so ridiculous that we'd burst out laughing and go to bed. And let me tell you, Doctor, for a man who has never had sex combined with love, it was and remains a wonderful experience.

After a few weeks of this, I told her that I desperately wanted to marry her if she would have me, but that in any case I was going to get a divorce. Having seen what life could be like, that my fantasies were not just that, I could not continue to live in that house and breathe. So she said she would, and that's what we are planning to do.

THERAPIST: And you asked your wife for a divorce?

DR. FURLONG: Yes, about three months ago.

THERAPIST: Her reaction?

DR. FURLONG: Angry, what else? But listen, I can see our time is almost up anyway, and I have to run. This is good. When can I see you again? Next time I want to show you something.

When Dr. Furlong came back for his second session, he was carrying a brown grocery bag. He sat down and pulled a shoe out of the sack. Turning it over, he said, "See this?" and pointed to a spot near the toe where the leather had worn thin.

DR. FURLONG: If a picture is worth a thousand words, a shoe is worth at least ten thousand. That's from grinding my big toe all day long. I used to have to replace or resole them three times a year at least. Chronic tension—living in a home without love for over thirty-five years. She was never happy, always angry. Walking on eggs . . . learned never to ask for anything . . . anticipate and head off any source of friction—that was married life.

Dr. FURLONG: That's my answer to your question, Doctor. Of course she was angry when I asked for a divorce, but no more so than early on when I asked for a kiss or, God forbid, sex.

Since meeting Elise, I don't punish my shoes any more, Doctor, and I'm not going back!

THERAPIST: As if I'm telling you to do so.

DR. FURLONG: (*Realizing how angry he has become*) You're right. I wonder why I did that? You have been helpful; I left last time feeling calm. I looked forward to coming here, but for a moment there I felt furious with you.

THERAPIST: I wonder, too. You sounded not just angry but defensive. If it's not me, who are you talking to? Who is standing in your way?

DR. FURLONG: I don't know. I don't feel angry now.

THERAPIST: You describe your married life as such a hell, but something moved you to marry your wife. And, let's not forget, you stayed in the marriage for thirty-five years.

DR. FURLONG: Believe me, I have thought about that in one way or another every day of those thirty-five years. As best as I have been able to figure it out, I sort of drifted into the marriage. Certainly when we were engaged I never had the feeling for her that I have for Elise. No, I would not say I was even in love with her when we got married.

THERAPIST: How did you meet and, as you say, drift into marriage?

DR. FURLONG: (*His expression becoming pensive and a half-smile playing around his mouth*) I come from poor people: shanty—not lace-curtain—Irish, if you know what that means. My dad worked on the docks—alcoholic, like the others, but he had ambitions for me. He wanted me to be a lawyer. He was a precinct captain on the side, and the only big-shots he knew were the aldermen and the fixers; all of them were lawyers, so that's what he wanted for me. I was never keen on it, but you didn't say no to Da. So, after high school, when he got me a summer job with the Man, the one who ran the machine, I went. I was lucky: Mr. Traynor took a shine to me, and when he saw me in the office he'd engage me in conversation that was more than superficial. I think we found each other; I was the son he never had, and he was the father I needed at that point, someone who would understand and guide me the way my own dad never could.

It became pretty obvious that, though I was a hard and willing worker, and a bright boy, the law and I were not meant for each other. I don't know how he figured it out, but one day he just sat me down and said that, from his observation, I'd make a better doctor than a lawyer. Then it all came together for me. He was right; Da's single-minded insistence on law had not let me think about what I really wanted to do. So Mr. Traynor—to this day I have to struggle to think of him as Patrick—said he would talk to Da and see what could be done. Of course there was no problem; Pat Traynor's word was law in the city and in every Irish home. He saw to it that I got a scholarship and, when I did well, there was no question but that I had a place in the state medical school. In those days it wasn't so easy to get in . . .

THERAPIST: And how. I remember—seven or more qualified applicants for every place.

DR. FURLONG: That's how it was. He was like a second father. Not like my Da—loud, blustering, falling down drunk, and making a fool of himself—but dignified, quiet, very serious, didn't smile much, but always seemed to know what was needed and got it done. We never had much, and the odds were that when we did have a little extra Da would drink it up. But now when I needed more money than I could earn working on the side and during vacations it materialized somehow. We never talked about it, but I'm sure Mr. Traynor gave it to Da, who, much as he might have liked to, would never have dared use it for anything other than what Mr. Traynor intended it to be used for.

He had me over for dinner quite a bit, and that's where I met her. She was his daughter, his only child. Sometimes I think maybe he had it all planned . . . but then I don't want to think that it was so, that I was manipulated like a puppet on a string. No, I don't believe that. Not that he wouldn't have thought of me as a prospect for Roseanne, but I have to believe he liked me for myself. I know he did.

As I told you, I don't think I fell in love with Roseanne—or she with me, for that matter—but we seemed to get along all right. She was not demanding. There isn't much time for socializing in a medical student's life—I don't have to explain that to you—and she never seemed put out when I had to cancel a date because there was a test—there were always tests—or showed up for dinner late. What I only later realized was that she was just as glad not to have to go out or have me around. Her father was the only man in her life. She knew he wanted her safely married before he went, and since I had his approval she drifted into it, as did I . . . I told you that before, didn't I?

I think the day we got married was the happiest day in Pat Traynor's life. Da and Mom were overcome with the honor. Da was either so intimidated or intoxicated by this social elevation by proxy that he stayed pleasant and sober for the entire week of the wedding, an earth-shaking event never to be repeated to the day he died—not of cirrhosis, by the way; a crate came down on him when he was in the hold, unloading.

The only ones not overcome with delight were Roseanne and I. We were doing what we were meant to do and maybe assumed that what everybody seemed to feel was right would turn out all right. But far from blossoming, what had been lukewarm affection soured almost immediately. She became very much like her mother—a nasty bitch, the exact opposite of Patrick—concerned only with how things looked and incapable of responding emotionally. I'd always wondered how Patrick tolerated his wife. Maybe he loved her; maybe it was inertia and the foolish hope that things couldn't get worse and had to get better. For the first few years that's how I felt. I was starting a practice, and so it helped that we had a nice house and no financial worries. Pat had settled a lot of money on her and made it clear to both of us that while he was alive anything we needed would be forthcoming and that after he and his wife were gone everything would go to her.

I guess I felt an obligation to her, even though, as I told you, when I started to do well it was my money that supported us and still does. Hers goes to the charities, and the ballet, and you name it. She is on more boards—"boughten friendship," as Frost calls it.

THERAPIST: "Provide, provide!"

DR. FURLONG: I used to get furious at having to go to those dinners and dances—everybody kissing everybody else "hello" and "good-bye"—a real love fest, when you knew damned well that the only thing that counted was your money. But when I learned to spot the unhappily married ladies at these functions, it made it less difficult to put on my tuxedo. No more need for that now— or ever, thank God. And then I couldn't hurt Pat; we remained best friends till the day he died. I never complained to him. I think he knew that things were not great, but he had lived with it and maybe felt that there was no other way; I've always believed that my loyalty meant a great deal to him.

THERAPIST: You had children.

DR. FURLONG: Oh, yes, we had to produce grandchildren, and we did: two girls that she managed to turn against me. She wouldn't let me have anything to do with them when they were little and then made me out to be an absentee father. One is in law school now; the other's in college and doesn't know yet what she'll do. My divorcing their mother just confirms their opinion of me. Neither one has called to hear my side of the story since their mother told them. I wanted us to tell them together, but of course Roseanne jumped the gun, and they don't seem interested in what I have to say.

THERAPIST: Yet though your wife, according to what you tell me, is not at all happy with you, your seeking a divorce made her angry.

DR. FURLONG: (*So carried away he apparently does not hear me*) We live in that big house, the two of us, and can spend days without saying anything to each other. I mean it, not a word. Not even "good morning" or "good night."

THERAPIST: And yet you say your wife is angered by the idea of divorce.

DR. FURLONG: To the world of charity balls, the opera, and the symphony, we are a couple. What will it look like to her society friends? What will people say? I took some pleasure in telling Roseanne that I didn't really care what her phony friends said. As long as she doesn't run out of money—and that's as likely as the sun rising in the west—those sycophants and toadies will continue to flatter and lionize her. As far as I'm concerned, she can put the blame on me—male menopause, good old Don Pasquale without the happy ending. I have paid my dues—no more!

THERAPIST: You don't have to convince me. You are the one who has to believe that you are entitled to take the steps that you are planning to take.

DR. FURLONG: You do believe me, don't you?

THERAPIST: Yes, I believe you, but I can't give you absolution. That's what you seem to be looking for. But whom have you offended, who are you afraid to hurt?

DR. FURLONG: I don't feel guilty, but you're right. I guess I do protest too much. Why I don't know.

By the end of this second session, I had the impression that the patient's anxiety was related to a sense of betraying an obligation to his deceased father-in-law, a conflict in the sector of attachment development. I did not become specific about my hunch, however. I suspected that given his capacity for introspection and access to his underlying feelings and emotions, he himself would come to that conclusion, unless he surprised me with some unforeseen data that might further clarify what was going on. And indeed, Dr. Furlong came into his third session looking relaxed and quite pleased with himself. He said he had had a dream about me. The setting was just as it is in reality: We were sitting across from each other, and he was talking to me about his determination to divorce Roseanne. But gradually my face, which had been pleasant enough at the outset, became increasingly distressed and changed into that of Patrick Traynor. He woke up at that point and realized he was crying.

The meaning of the dream seemed clear enough to him: His marriage to Roseanne was a gift of love to the only person—until he met Elise—who he felt both understood him and cared enough to do something about it. Now that Pat was dead, he felt guilty about going back on his promise to love, honor, and obey—not Roseanne, but her father.

DR. FURLONG: If I was going to leave her, I should have been a man and done it when Pat was alive.

THERAPIST: At that time there was no Elise.

DR. FURLONG: No, there never was anyone I cared for. A lot were compliant, some were exciting, some said they loved me, but I never felt that love myself.

But I've been thinking about what you said: absolution. I have to absolve myself, and I think I have. I thought back on it, and I think I've given you the wrong impression. I made it sound as if I was hopping in and out of women's beds from day one. That is not the way it was. For nine years I tried to make a go of it and didn't fool around. I told you that I had to beg for a kiss or some sex, but you have to understand—no, you don't have to understand, I have to remember—this was not an occasional thing. For nine years not a day passed when I didn't try to show Roseanne that our lives could be different, that if we both tried to work on the relationship something could grow. After all, for most of history, marriages were arranged, often still are, and that enforced intimacy has, I'm sure, led to—I don't know if you'd call it love in the romantic sense, but something more mutually satisfying than we had. But all I got back was the sound of one hand clapping. Then the kids were born, and instead of getting better, things got worse. That's when I went on the prowl and figured I had to get something back.

THERAPIST: Why do you think you started looking around after your daughters were born? Why then?

DR. FURLONG: I've thought about that. Maybe it was then that the hope was destroyed that children would make a difference and that we could still have a life—some fantasy that the bitterness, the disappointment, and the anger could somehow be reversed. As it turned out—I told you—my children have precious little affection for me, or need, for that matter. Their trust funds make them totally independent of the usual financial apron strings that tie children to their father, but I didn't feel that way about them. When they were born I felt the bond very keenly; I could no more have up and left them than I could have jumped over the moon. That she didn't let me be the father I might have been did not change my sense of responsibility to these girls. They did not ask to be born into a dysfunctional family. But I also knew I could not endure the marital desert much longer. So I figured if I could not have love, I could give and take physical pleasure and the momentary affection that comes with it. I never kidded myself that it was love, but I will say I never had sex casually or with prostitutes; the women I went with—usually for months and, in one case, for several years—were people I had some feeling for and who cared for me. I guess you might say I had extramarital affairs to make the continuation of my marriage possible, for the girls' sake.

THERAPIST: And perhaps to make it unnecessary for you to leave and have to face Pat with your decision—if he was still alive then.

DR. FURLONG: You've got a good point there. Yes, he was still alive, very much so. He went at eighty-six, had a coronary at work, died instantly. Must be ten years now.

THERAPIST: So now you have to wrestle with your conscience.

DR. FURLONG: That I have done in the last week since I saw you. I am grateful to Patrick, and I will never forget him, but I do not owe him my life. I made my decision to divorce before I came to see you, but now I think I can live with it comfortably. My anger at Roseanne seems to have turned to pity. She's a victim, too; she must have envisioned a different life, too. The kids—I don't know—I'll do what I can. Maybe if I can let myself be happier—happy—it will change our relationship somewhere down the road.

THERAPIST: That would not be unusual at all.

DR. FURLONG: I would hope Pat could have forgiven me, but it's more important that I have forgiven myself.

THERAPIST: One can do that once the name of the game and the identity of the players is clear.

DR. FURLONG: I'm grateful to you for that. I owe you a lot. (*Pauses*) This is amazing . . .

THERAPIST: Mmm?

DR. FURLONG: It never occurred to me to call any other psychiatrist; I just found your number and picked up the phone.

THERAPIST: Yes?

DR. FURLONG: That seminar you gave to the medicine department—it must be five, six years ago?

THERAPIST: Sure.

DR. FURLONG: I was there . . .

THERAPIST: I know, I remember.

DR. FURLONG: I had forgotten all about it till now. But now I remember, and you know, your way of talking—or maybe it's the three-piece suits you always wear—made me think of Pat. I think you really are a lot like him.

THERAPIST: So there was the possibility of absolution here when you still thought you needed it.

DR. FURLONG: It always turns out that Freud was right, doesn't it? What a phenomenon.

THERAPIST: He is indeed.

DR. FURLONG: I should read some Freud. I've read about him, but there's never a substitute for the real McCoy, is there?

THERAPIST: Very true—especially true for Freud.

DR. FURLONG: Maybe I'll read the dream book, or those Introductory Lectures. They're in paperback.

THERAPIST: I wouldn't start there. The titles are deceptive. Those can be difficult and confusing works. If you want a straightforward account of what Freud thought analysis was about, read *The Question of Lay Analysis*. That really is an introductory lecture.

DR. FURLONG: Good, thanks. And thanks again for helping me sort all this out. I'll be back if I need to be.

THERAPIST: Fine, and good luck.

Dr. Furlong illustrates a type of patient often described in textbooks but seldom encountered in practice. These patients, with the support of the positive transference, engage in a narrative that orients them and in the process lets them resolve their difficulties. My function was only to guide and validate. What had been an unresolved attachment issue came to be dealt with successfully in the sector of autonomy. As usually happens, once he was able to grow up and accept the necessity of living with the import of his decision, his anxiety was relieved. Additionally, and not unexpectedly, once Dr. Furlong took responsibility for himself, the rage at his wife subsided and was replaced by a more empathic perception.

The reason why Dr. Furlong was able to progress so rapidly was that whatever unconscious shame or guilt he was experiencing did not make him resistant to introspection. As will be discussed in the next chapter, these are the primary obstacles that stand in the way of brief psychotherapy.

CHAPTER 7

When More Time Is Needed to Achieve Character Change: Michelle Longwood

SHORT-TERM TREATMENT is not recommended when (1) it becomes clear that the patient will need prolonged support to be able to continue functioning competently, (2) the patient's resistances are such that the therapist will not be able to arrive at a satisfactory orientation to the problem without extensive investigation, or (3) the patient's deficits are of such a nature and/or of such an extent that substantial development and growth can occur only within a transference relationship. A diagnostic interview conducted according to the developmental model can usually establish fairly quickly not only whether a patient needs long-term treatment but also why.

THE NEED FOR PROLONGED SUPPORT

Michelle Longwood, a forty-two-year-old physician, sought psychiatric assistance for problems related to multiple addictions: food, alcohol, and narcotics. She felt that her psychological decompensation was related to the terminal illness and recent death of her husband.

The patient was the only child of a well-to-do couple who lived in a suburb of Chicago. Highly intelligent and painfully introspective, she knew herself to have been a fearful child who felt comfortable only within walking distance of her parents. The very idea of attending an overnight camp, participating in a pajama party, or visiting a friend's summer home for a few days was so anxiety-provoking that such outings were never even attempted. An industrious and accomplished student, she did well in grammar and high school. She could have gone to a top-flight college, but she chose a lesser institution that permitted her to live at home. Although being a physician appealed to her, her choice of medicine as a career was also influenced by the fact that admission to any one of the four medical colleges in Chicago would permit her to continue living with her parents; of course, she applied to no schools outside her hometown. She married a fellow student, not primarily for his many good qualities and his love for her, she said, but because her parents were getting older and she feared being left alone.

The marriage apparently was a reasonably happy one. Dr. Longwood and her husband, both pediatricians, established a flourishing practice together and, when their own children were born, arranged their professional schedules so as to share the task of raising them. As long as the patient felt supported, she functioned on a high level. She was a competent physician and an effective mother; she had many friends and was active in the community. Even her mother's death and, shortly thereafter, her father's confinement in a nursing home due to premature senility did not lead her to decompensate psychologically. Dr. Longwood's stability began to be undermined, however, when her husband was diagnosed as suffering from a rare bone cancer. As the disease progressed, she nursed her husband faithfully and with compassion. She maintained her professional life and, with the assistance of her full-time housekeeper, cared for the children. But she felt increasingly anxious during the day and could hardly sleep at night. No matter how much she tried to tell herself that the reality of her daily life belied her fears, she pictured herself as incapable of carrying on once her husband was gone. Driven by anxiety, she began to overeat. When she gained so much weight that she could no longer fit into her clothes, she tried unsuccessfully to control her anxiety and insomnia by taking first small then increasingly large amounts of the narcotics prescribed for her husband. She sought no help, because she feared that if her condition became known she would put her professional reputation in jeopardy and possibly lose her license to practice medicine. When she added alcohol abuse to her desperate search for relief, her deterioration became increasingly obvious. Her husband, though desperately ill and in severe pain, nevertheless kept his wits about him and, with the help of several of their close friends, forced her to face her condition. She agreed to be hospitalized anonymously, so that she could be withdrawn from alcohol and narcotics and begin psychological treatment.

Once in the treatment center Dr. Longwood participated in group therapy and soon became the star patient. In compliance with the program, she went to Alcoholics Anonymous (AA) and a similar program for drug-addicted people. She was released from the hospital prior to completing the full program because her husband was in the final stages of his illness. He died two weeks after she returned home. With the help of friends, her AA sponsor, and members of the drug support group, she coped quite well with the loss of her spouse. Although she was now free of chemical dependence, several months after winding up her husband's affairs she consulted a psychiatrist who had been previously recommended to her, to continue the psychological treatment begun in the hospital.

When her therapist consulted me about her case, Dr. Longwood had been in twice-weekly therapy for about a month. In her first visit to the office, what had been most noticeable was her eagerness to please the therapist. She volunteered her history, took appropriate pride in her sobriety and freedom from drugs, but acknowledged that food was still a problem for her. She was at that point still significantly overweight, but she assured the therapist—as if he had admonished her—that she would now join a weight-loss program. True to her word, she had done just that, was adhering to the prescribed diet, and was losing a pound or two a week. Right from the beginning, the patient had behaved as if therapy was now a permanent part of her life. In the initial interview, she asked about the therapist's vacation times so she might coordinate her time off with his. She wanted to know when and if he increased his fees periodically, so that she might plan for that in her budget.

What troubled the therapist and led to his consultation with me was the feeling that therapy was contributing nothing of value. In each session, Dr. Longwood seemed content to tell him how well things were going: She was attending all her support group meetings, remaining abstinent, gradually resuming her professional work, handling the children well during this difficult emotional time, and so on. As the therapist attempted to probe deeper into Dr. Longwood's childhood history to gain insight into the source of her separation anxiety, the patient would answer questions politely, listen seemingly attentively to whatever the therapist had to say, and then use any opportunity to resume her tale of the events of her everyday life and the evidence of her ever-increasing improvement. It seemed that nothing more was to be gained; at least at present, the patient seemed incapable of going deeper and exploring the roots of her psychological difficulties. Simply providing her with an audience would hardly be called psychotherapy; indeed, the therapist felt it was almost unprofessional to let the patient keep coming under such circumstances. Knowing of my interest in short-term treatment, he wanted to know whether to draw the therapy to a close—or rather, how to go about bringing this sort of treatment to a natural end.

My view of the case was quite different from that of Dr. Longwood's therapist. In terms of the sectors of development, the difficulty seemed to lie in the area of autonomy; there was a life-long history in which competence depended on ongoing attachment. The idealizing transference was strong and was present from the beginning of therapy. What the patient appeared to be looking for was the validating response of the therapist. As long as attachment was secure, the patient's problem-solving capacity was excellent; she was well oriented to her situation and its potential problems, had developed and was continuing to develop excellent coping skills, successfully maintained good relationships with her friends and within her support groups, and made good affective contact in therapy. Her ability to reflect on her situation and organize it in a coherent narrative was shown both in her being the star in group therapy and in the manner in which she presented herself to her therapist.

Yet this was not a short-term treatment case, I felt, even though the patient was no longer addicted and had successfully reentered her family and professional life. What Dr. Longwood was trying to do now was to engage the therapist in the validating aspect of the positive transference. I suspected that if her therapy were terminated now, she would rapidly decompensate and be unable to cope with the recent loss of her husband, who had answered her attachment needs until the therapist entered her life. Her ability to turn readily from her parents, first to her husband and now to the therapist, was not, to me, a sign of shallowness or lack of emotional capacity but an effective compensatory mechanism for what seemed to be lacking in the sector of autonomy. The analogy that came to my mind as I heard about this patient was to a child who comes home from school with "Guess what happened today?" The child wants to be debriefed, as it were, and supported by the parents' validating interest in schoolday activities. When parents hear about what the teacher said and who did what to whom in the playground, and when they take pride in a good grade or share a disappointment, these events take on a reality for the child that they did not have before. They become really real and can then become integrated into the child's self. Similarly, patients like Dr. Longwood need ongoing feedback from the parental other. That her therapist was listening patiently and with interest was very helpful, but it was not enough. I recommended that, like the parent who shows an interest in the child's day at school, the therapist not only listen but inquire about the details of what happened. For example, if I were Dr. Longwood's therapist, I would want to know the names of the members of the support group, and I would ask who responded to her, and what Bill had to say, and whether Mary made her usual cynical comment, and so on. Validation—or mirroring—does not mean primarily echoing or approving, although these also may have their place, but involves actively coming to know the details of the patient's transactions with those around her. The validity of her existence rests on the interest of the significant other. The reason the therapist felt useless was that he was frustrated by being unable to get to the bottom of the patient's need.

I think of all psychotherapy as consisting of three potential phases: restoring the cohesive self, strengthening and maintaining the cohesive self, and then working with the patient to gain insight into the structure of the self. With many patients the restoration of the cohesive self is all that is needed, and these are of course the patients who benefit from short-term treatment. Psychoanalytic work is done primarily in the third phase, during which the emphasis is on gaining insight into sequestered aspects of the patient's unconscious. With patients like Dr. Longwood, the focus is on the second phase, the maintenance of a viable self. Dr. Longwood came to the therapist with an already restored cohesive self, thanks to the intervention of her friends, the treatment center, and the support groups. The therapist's job was now to maintain and strengthen the cohesive self through appropriate validation. Whether or not the third phase would be engaged remained to be seen; but that phase should be broached only when the patient signals readiness and ability to take this step.

Historically, dynamic therapy has been equated with the third step, helping the patient achieve insight into the formation of the self through judicious interpretation of the hints signaled by the unconscious. But this is too narrow a definition. As I have said in an earlier publication (1988), dynamic psychotherapy encompasses everything therapists do to free the patient to make those decisions that will most likely lead to competence (recall figure 1.2). Interpretation—that is, making the unconscious conscious—is one way of promoting this outcome, but it is not the only way. Dr. Longwood's case required the therapist's validation of the patient's successful effort to sustain competence and the accompanying sense of accomplishment and well-deserved self-esteem, and that would necessitate an open-ended treatment. I suggested to Dr. Longwood's therapist that once he was able to recognize the legitimacy of the patient's need and understand the necessity of ongoing therapy at this level, he would find this to be as gratifying and instructive a therapy as those in which exploring childhood and establishing the underlying reasons for a patient's behavior are focal. Many patients like Dr. Longwood, given the therapist's appropriate validation of their efforts to achieve competence, eventually gain the strength to stand on their own. They then find that therapy has served its purpose and can be ended. Termination for these patients usually involves a gradual tapering off of the frequency of sessions and then an explicit agreement that treatment can be resumed when and if it is needed.

RESISTANCE

The second group of patients who do not lend themselves to short-term treatment includes those who want and need help but whose guilt, mistrust, or shame stands in the way of appropriate orientation to their difficulties; without orientation to the problem, the next steps toward resolution cannot be taken (see figure 1.3). The guilt-ridden patients described by Freud provide us with the classic example of this sort of situation.

We tend to forget that Freud began his career in psychiatry doing brief psychotherapy. For at least ten years, from 1887 to 1897, he used hypnosis to age-regress his patients, so that the precipitating event of their pathology could be identified and the associated traumatic memories relived and relieved through countersuggestion and abreaction. These treatments were completed in a matter of weeks, but as Freud learned, initial success in symptom removal did not necessarily mean that the patient was cured. A certain number of patients relapsed, and repeated hypnotic treatments proved to have no more lasting effects than the first. The psychoanalytic method gradually evolved as Freud and these patients, for whose pathology he coined the term *psychoneurosis,* struggled to find a more enduring answer for their difficulties (Gay 1988; Jones 1953).

What Freud learned and taught us was that in the case of psychoneurotic patients, therapy could not make a direct link between childhood trauma and the manifest symptomatology of the patient. The patient's guilt about forbidden sexual desires of childhood stood in the way of insight and abreaction. Only as the forbidden sexual desire—the oedipal conflict—was remobilized bit by bit in the relationship to the analyst, relived, and this time interpreted rather than punitively dealt with, could the patient's guilt be obviated sufficiently to let the precipitating events or fantasies emerge.

Similarly, Heinz Kohut, using the psychoanalytic method of transference analysis, found that patients who early in life have been deprived of appropriate validation become ashamed—not of their affective needs, but of themselves for having those needs. And because of that shame, these patients may for a long time resist letting their needs emerge in therapy. A long period of what Kohut (1971) called *empathic immersion* is required as these patients make the vicissitudes of the therapeutic relationship per se the therapeutic issue. Only when they work through their shame vis-à-vis their need for the therapist can they permit themselves to repeat in the transference what happened in their early formative years. Here again, therapy must be open-ended. (I have discussed elsewhere [1988] the diagnosis and treatment of psychoneurotic problems and narcissistic personality disorders.)

ARRESTED OR SKEWED DEVELOPMENT

A third group of patients who need more than short-term therapy consists of patients whose developmental deficit is readily apparent, but who then need the opportunity to grow up, as it were, in the therapeutic relationship. This step is what Freud called *Nacherziehung,* or belated upbringing. In the treatment of these patients, as in short-term therapy, the therapist is active and the therapy is progressive rather than regressive, but the time frame is different. These patients need an open-ended therapy in which the therapist not only conveys understanding of their emotional needs but guides them in the fulfillment of those needs.

Adolescent patients fall into this category, as do some patients who are newly married or facing some other dramatic change in their accustomed life situation (Basch 1980, 1988). It is important not to come to premature conclusions, however. Sometimes a patient with significant developmental issues will respond amazingly quickly to short-term treatment. Mr. Dale was such a one.

The received wisdom has been that we can best serve our patients by helping them understand the influence of childhood events on their present difficulties as they relive their past in the transference to the therapist. Anything short of such necessarily lengthy treatment is seen as a compromise. I recommend a 180 degree turn. Think of every patient as someone who until proven otherwise can be helped to use what that person has built up in the way of competence to resolve the problem, whatever it may be. The application of the developmental model will very quickly identify those relatively few patients who require more than brief therapy. In those cases, what we have learned can be used to help the patients understand not only that they need lengthier treatment but why it is necessary.

III

Brief Psychotherapy and Limited Goals

CHAPTER 8

Clarification and Guidance: Grant Rausen and William Semic

THE PATIENTS we have been considering up to this point were motivated for psychotherapy and were ready and able to discuss the nature and course of their respective problems as they understood them. The clinical cases that follow provide the opportunity to see how one can deal productively, albeit in limited fashion, with patients who are less able to participate in the therapeutic process. They demonstrate that even with patients who are unable to bond with and/or rely on others, judicious use of the developmental model can usually overcome this handicap sufficiently to produce a significant therapeutic outcome.

GRANT RAUSEN

The first patient I discuss in this part was far from eager to see a therapist, and though ultimately his developmental issues were most instructive, initially he presented quite a challenge. How to deal with him remained a puzzle for some time.

Session 1

When I greeted Grant Rausen, a balding, somewhat paunchy forty-year-old man, I thought his response was a bit too hearty; it struck me as being false. He came into the office carrying a medium-sized ring binder, and even though there is an end table next to the patient's chair for just such items, he did not put his notebook down throughout the session. His suit jacket seemed tight on him, but he kept it buttoned. I got the impression that he was doing his best to insulate himself.

Mr. Rausen said he had been told that he had a problem with communication and should resign his position. He was outraged that this should be his reward for fifteen years of dedicated and effective service to his employer, a department store chain for which he worked at the middle-management level. He had filed a grievance and been given a hearing. The arbitrator who heard the case had ruled that he could either resign and receive six months' severance pay or else continue to work and have psychotherapy at the expense of the company, to see if his problem could be resolved. If he chose the latter course and his performance evaluation did not improve in six months, his employer would be free to discharge him.

As he told me this story, Mr. Rausen might have been talking about someone else. There was no fear in his voice; on the contrary, he sounded supremely self-assured, as if he were in no difficulty whatsoever. He went on to tell me that he completely rejected the evaluation he had been given. He went to great lengths, he said, to keep open the lines of communication between himself and his colleagues. It was his manager, Roger Bennan, who created the problems, not he. There was no way of pleasing the man. When Mr. Rausen asked for clarification and direction, Roger did not give it to him. When he asked for help, Roger had no time for him or did the job himself. Until two years ago, when Roger was placed in charge of his department, no one had complained about him. Mr. Rausen said that he understood very well what was going on: He was being set up to be the fall guy. Roger Bennan was afraid that the vice president would judge their department to be deficient and was looking for a scapegoat.

Mr. Rausen said he could see no point in coming to see me; he had agreed to an appointment only to avoid being dismissed immediately. He anticipated that sometime soon he would get to see the vice president, and he was certain that once he explained the situation and reviewed his record with her, she would rule in his favor.

With every prospective patient one has to make a decision as to whether or not psychotherapy is indicated, and this might very well have been a person for whom it was not. What struck me was Mr. Rausen's demeanor. His attitude signaled an absence of any sense of kinship with me. Even if he had been sent to the wrong place, I would expect some eagerness to enlist me on his side and get confirmation for his viewpoint. Mr. Rausen, however, did not seem to care what I thought and wanted nothing from me. If indeed he was correct in his belief that he didn't belong in my office, we could simply part company. But if there was a need for psychotherapy here, this seeming lack of any awareness that he might require and could use my help would prove to be a problem.

As I listened to Mr. Rausen, I became increasingly uncomfortable. He spoke in an unctuous, sanctimonious, holier-than-thou tone that put my teeth on edge. Also, I have learned to distrust self-righteous statements that leave no room for any other point of view except the speaker's own. I could, of course, not dismiss the possibility that he was correct in his assessment of the situation; people do get scapegoated. So, in the interest of collecting more information, I asked him to tell me about his job: What exactly did he do? Perhaps, I suggested, he could also give me an example of a project he had completed successfully and contrast it with one in which he could have used Roger's help, had the latter been willing to give it to him.

What happened then was most revealing. Mr. Rausen became eager to comply and spoke at some length. The problem was that what he said made no sense at all, and I really mean no sense. I don't think I sat there with my mouth hanging open, but that is how I felt. Trying to follow what he was saying was not just disconcerting; it was impossible. His sentences were on the order of "Do you take the bus to New York or do you carry your lunch?" The words were arranged grammatically and formed sentences, but the end product was totally meaningless. When I managed to pick out some phrase that seemed to have some potential for coherence and asked for clarification, Mr. Rausen only muddied the waters further. I now thought I understood what was likely to be behind his employer's attempt to dismiss him. Yet, on the asset side, it seemed to me that he could not have been totally confused and confusing throughout the years; he had performed well enough to have held his job and been promoted to his present position.

Here was a situation in which goal setting was going to be a problem. Mr. Rausen's goal in coming to therapy was only to comply with the letter of the arbitrator's recommendation. At this point I still had no idea whether Mr. Rausen could be engaged in therapy or what, if anything, I might be able to do to help him.

Knowing that continued direct confrontation of his incoherence would in all probability prove to be futile, I switched tactics and asked him to tell me about his family and his earlier years. He immediately became coherent. This was an important sign, indicating to me that his propensity for word salad when describing his problematic work life was probably a way of trying to cope with the anxiety precipitated by the subject of his work situation. That is, what was happening or not happening in relation to his manager, Roger Bennan, threatened to be so disorganizing that emergency measures were called for. The best he had been able to do to ward off the fear that accompanies the threat of major disorganization was to generate a caricature of an explanation—a testament to the degree of stress to which he felt subjected. I had been afraid that perhaps there was a failure of kinship across the board, that he had become so isolated from others that he no longer had any hope of making himself understood and essentially carried on monologues that were not meant to be communications. I was encouraged to find that this was not so; if the anxiety aroused by any discussion of his work situation could be ameliorated, his difficulties could become much clearer.

In the course of his narrative, I learned that Grant was the fifth of nine siblings; he had five brothers and three sisters. His father was a part-time preacher who also ran a hardware store in a small town in Iowa; his mother worked in the store. His childhood, as he recalled it, was one of emotional and material deprivation. He always felt that his parents were too harassed by the care of their large family to invest themselves emotionally in its individual members. His parents enforced discipline by shaming; any misbehaving child was held up to ridicule. Banishment for even minor infractions of the family rules was common. There was no closeness among the brothers and sisters; they turned on one another at the first opportunity and fought continually. As adults, they had little to do with one another. The only one to whom he felt close was a sister, three years older, who took a quasi-maternal interest in him. After this sister's marriage broke up, she turned to drugs and alcohol, and Grant had helped her as much as he could.

He enlisted in the army after graduating from high school and found himself assigned as a combination secretary and research assistant to an officer at the War College. This man took an interest in him and encouraged him to enroll in the evening program of a nearby university. Three years later Grant successfully completed his course work and was awarded an Associate in Arts degree. He thought of that time as the happiest of his life. When his mentor was transferred, Grant lost interest in an army career and left the service. After his discharge, he parlayed his experience into a job in the research library of a pharmaceutical company and then used the employee benefit plan to pursue a degree in library science. His interest in the field waned, however, and he switched to a business curriculum. After receiving an M.B.A., he changed jobs and began working for his present employer. My ears perked up, as did my spirits, when I heard Mr. Rausen's history. It showed a capacity for reliance and an ability to benefit from a relationship when it was offered in a way he could use.

Mr. Rausen was not married, but he had an ongoing relationship with a woman ten years older than he, one of his former teachers in business school. Although they maintained separate apartments, they spent vacations and most weekends together. Since neither of them wanted children, the question of marriage, though it came up periodically, had never gone further; they both seemed to value their independence. This was another bit of evidence on the plus side. Mr. Rausen could maintain and gain from an ongoing relationship if the level of intimacy was within comfortable limits.

Like Warren Dale, Grant Rausen seemed to have been significantly traumatized in the attachment sector of development, but he had adapted to emotional deprivation in quite a different way. Warren Dale had retained an affective flexibility that permitted him to be much more forthcoming than Grant Rausen, who was more isolated and unable to communicate effectively when under stress. Yet, when one added up his assets and liabilities, Mr. Rausen's capacity to take and follow advice that made sense to him was a definite plus.

Almost as an afterthought, Mr. Rausen added that he had begun drinking at the age of sixteen and soon became an alcoholic. For years he fooled himself into thinking he had no problem because he always functioned effectively, though he drank himself into oblivion most nights. About five years ago, he found himself having memory lapses, and the physician he consulted told him that if he continued to drink as he was doing he would wind up either dead or a vegetable. He was advised to save himself by joining Alcoholics Anonymous (AA). Mr. Rausen took this advice and guidance to heart. He no longer consumed alcohol in any form, and he went to at least five AA meetings a week in the basement of a church near his home; in addition he often skipped lunch and used the time to attend the noon meetings held not far from his office. As he told me about his conversion to sobriety, he showed some animation for the first time, but soon his tone became zealous and his manner patronizing and unctuous. He lectured me on the purpose of AA, described how meetings were run, and outlined the program's twelve steps. The idea that as a psychiatrist I could have treated other patients with alcohol problems and might well be familiar with AA never seemed to occur to him. He told me that, in keeping with the program, whenever possible he had done what he could to make amends to all those whom he might have injured in the past. Now he wanted to embark on a course of forgiving those who had injured him. He planned to begin with his siblings and his parents.

I suspected that Mr. Rausen's alcoholism might well have begun as a response to the loneliness of an adolescent who was bereft of emotional support, and I considered it one more demonstration of an inner strength in the pursuit of competence that he was now able to put an end to his self-destructive behavior by replacing a chemical addiction with reliance on the kinship of AA. The desperate dependence was still evident, but dependence on other people and a shared vision could prove to be a gateway to maturity, while reliance on alcohol is a dead end. Although I continued to find myself put off by his self-satisfied presentation, I could appreciate how far he had come and how much he had been able to accomplish, given the damage that had been inflicted upon him. As the end of the session approached, I said to Mr. Rausen that as yet I had no specific comments to make and suggested we continue to meet on a weekly basis and explore his situation. "I'm a team player," he replied, and we scheduled the next appointment.

In this first session I had not succeeded in orienting myself sufficiently to establish a definitive goal for therapy, but I held on to the concept that, no matter how confused and confusing Mr. Rausen's attempt to clarify his problematic work situation might be, he was striving for competence, as we all do. Although he was failing miserably, one could only conclude that right now this was the best he could do. At least there was no generalized thought disorder. His incomprehensibility seemed to be limited to his attempt to his explanations of his professional activities; he spoke in a perfectly understandable manner in describing his early life, his relationship with his lover, and his struggle with alcoholism. I provisionally concluded that his gibberish was a defensive maneuver. Something had made him so anxious—that is, disorganized—that to deny the threat, whatever it might be, he substituted verbal activity—a pseudo-narrative—for what should have been more appropriate coping mechanisms.

Of course, one can also turn the situation around and observe that my evaluation of Mr. Rausen's strange behavior—my making sense out of what did not seem to make sense—was my way of quieting the anxiety that I began to experience when faced by the patient's garbled attempt at communication. I therefore qualified my hypothesis as provisional; only time and the experience of working further with the patient would let me know whether it would hold up. That is the way it always is in this business: Too much uncertainty makes us too anxious to function productively, and too much fear of anxiety can lead us to an ordering that is not productive. It was the latter mind-set that I attributed to Mr. Rausen, and I had to be careful not to fall into the same trap.

At the end of the first session, I saw Mr. Rausen's primary liability as an inability to step back and look at either himself or others with some objectivity, combined with a lack of flexibility in making a recovery when his competence was challenged. On the asset side, he had not been as damaged by his childhood experiences as he might have been; he responded well when interest was shown in him and was able to grow when directed in a manner he could accept. Until a few years ago, he must have performed well to reach his present position at work. He had been able to maintain a personal relationship, albeit a limited one, and he had been able to use help to control a severe addictive problem, substituting human support for chemical solutions. As in every case, the challenge was how to mobilize Mr. Rausen's assets and use them effectively.

From the perspective of the developmental spiral, this patient had made an unconscious decision to protect his self-esteem with the kind of double-talk that left him satisfied but everyone else confused and frustrated. Why would such an extreme measure be necessary? To judge from his history, Mr. Rausen did quite well when guided in a way he could understand and accept. Under the aegis of his mentor in the army, he was able to turn his life around; he succeeded in the structured atmosphere of the university and earned an advanced degree; his business career had been a successful one up to a point. Perhaps he was correct in thinking that his trouble began when he was given a new manager. But maybe the problem was not that his manager was plotting to undermine him but that there was some miscommunication between the two that did not permit Mr. Rausen to use his abilities to good effect. Of course, Mr. Rausen's inability to deal flexibly with this situation and adapt to the new regime was also an issue to be explained.

Given the definition of competence as the ability to meet one's needs in the context of adaptation to the environment, Mr. Rausen's situation was the opposite of the one that faced Mr. Dale. Mr. Dale functioned perfectly no matter how he was challenged, but his sense of self-worth was not enhanced by his performance. Mr. Rausen's self-esteem seemed to be intact, but at the cost of a maladaptation reflected in his performance, one that could have serious consequences.

Though I believed I understood the patient better, the specifics of how I might help him use his assets to resolve his difficulties continued to elude me. I did think that if I could learn more about the origin and nature of the miscommunication between Mr. Rausen and his manager, however, I would have a much better idea of where to go next with the therapy.

SESSIONS 2–3

Mr. Rausen reported that he had received written comments evaluating a meeting he had led. The participants said that he was judgmental and defensive. They suggested that he loosen up and relax, not be so uptight. When I asked how he reacted to these observations, he said he just got frustrated when nothing was accomplished. He then launched into a long, confused story about the nonproductive meetings his boss ran.

Mr. Rausen wanted to be seen as open-minded, warm, and caring, but he knew he was not seen that way at work. By contrast, he felt very gratified by what had happened in his Alcoholics Anonymous meeting. The other participants had noticed that he had become much freer emotionally. They told him that where "once he talked from the head, now he talks from the heart." He felt loved at AA.

This last was said in a smug but flat tone. It put me in mind of the protagonist of Richard Condon's novel *The Manchurian Candidate*, a man who had been brainwashed and functioned as an automaton. That is, Mr. Rausen's statement lacked the affective component that one would expect to accompany such a declaration. I was quite sure that, as in Mr. Dale's case, Mr. Rausen's early upbringing had resulted in an affective developmental deficit. The idea that intellectual capacity lags—or at least is likely to lag—without stimulation is generally accepted today. What is not so well known is that the same holds for the development of affect.

I commented on the patient's need for acceptance, and this idea seemed to make sense to him. For the first time in our sessions, he really looked at me, and he replied in an understandable and direct way, "I know I have problems, I always feel I have to prove myself; I never got recognition for what I did at home." Then he added, "My boss, my father, and I all have the same problem: We don't give credit the way it needs to be given."

I asked in what way he did not credit others appropriately. Mr. Rausen once more became vague: "I should relate better to the people in the office"; he could not give specific examples, even when I pressed him to do so. I took this response—or, rather, lack of response—as tending to confirm my hypothesis regarding his affective handicap. He mouthed affective platitudes, but they had no real meaning for him that he could express.

Mr. Rausen was hurt that his boss had marked the birthday of one of the secretaries in the office with flowers and congratulations, yet his birthday, a few weeks earlier, had not been acknowledged. He did not agree with my suggestion that his boss was probably not discriminating against him but rather treating him differently from the secretary because of the differences in their respective positions in the company. We should all be treated equally, he maintained. I wondered aloud whether this need for equal treatment might be related to his childhood and the need to compete with eight brothers and sisters for affection and attention. That suggestion only made him angry. "Why are you calling me a child?" he wanted to know. It was clear that what so often works did not do so here. Linking past emotional experiences to present ones did not help this patient. He was mollified by my apology in the form of a clarification of the comparison, but he understood the analogy no better.

Mr. Rausen then presented another injustice for consideration. His boss did not like to be interrupted, but he had no hesitation about interrupting Mr. Rausen when the latter was busy. I had a hard time believing what I had heard and said, half jokingly, "Your boss does not make appointments with you?"

"AA has taught me that we are all equal," Mr. Rausen said. "We are all human beings. I have no right to exercise power over others, and they have none over me." I pointed out that the office was not an AA meeting. In AA all are united and made equal by their ailment, but in the office a hierarchical situation is implicit. Mr. Rausen replied by reciting, from memory and as if it was a litany, a relevant paragraph from one of the steps in the Big Book, the bible of AA, that supported his position.

I was typing at the word processor a few weeks ago when a message came on the screen: "This document is contaminated." I attempted to right matters, but I could not even clear the window. Nothing I did had any effect on what I took as an accusatory message. I felt helpless and somewhat guilty. My attempts to assist Mr. Rausen felt like that to me. No matter which way I turned, nothing I did seemed to make any real difference. Like a deer caught in the headlights of an oncoming car, Mr. Rausen could not save himself and so far had given me no hint of how I might help him do so.

SESSIONS 4–9

Since Mr. Rausen felt reasonably comfortable in AA meetings, I encouraged him to tell me more about his participation in these meetings and to reflect on what it meant to him to belong to the group. In his response he dwelled on the care and concern the members had for one another. This thought then led him to tell me more about his childhood and the psychological deprivations he had endured. Not only was there no time for him, but he was expected to be perfect and to create no problems for his overworked mother. She had been only sixteen years old when she had her first child, and she had had eight more babies after that, one every other year. Several miscarriages then occurred, and a hysterectomy followed. Some weeks after the surgery his mother was taken back to the hospital—for treatment of a depression, Mr. Rausen thought. When she came back after a month, no one ever talked about it; life just went on as if nothing had happened. His mother always seemed exhausted and tired, both before the hysterectomy and afterward. I commented, "You never had your fair share of attention, then, and it sounds as if you still feel that way now at work."

"A light bulb just went on," he said, but he added that, since he had already talked about his childhood at AA meetings, there was no point in continuing to rehash that part of his life.

I then asked him about his previous manager, and from what he told me it became clear that this earlier relationship had met his need for reliance in a way he could use; like his mentor in the service, his previous boss had given him guidance in the context of the nurturing parental ambience for which he longed. I pointed out the difference between the present disappointment in his manager and the former supportive experience. The contrast was of no concern to him, he said. He felt good that he was helpful and supportive to the people under him, and he did not need recognition from his boss. He had learned in AA to give that to himself.

When Mr. Rausen was called in for his annual review, he was very disappointed to be given only a token raise in pay, although his boss said his work was good. "I busted my butt," he complained. Roger agreed that he worked very hard and blamed the vice president for the low increase in his salary. Mr. Rausen was angry that no one was telling him what was wrong or how he might improve. He was convinced that Roger said one thing to him and then undermined him with the vice president.

He did report that he felt his communication skills had improved. He was angry with his lover when she cancelled some weekend plans they had made, but he was able to speak about it with her, and they arrived at an amicable compromise. He noted that his anger went away as soon as he was able to start the discussion. This, as I explained to him, was a good demonstration that his anger was secondary to frustration, to an inability to function competently; as soon as he found himself behaving appropriately, his distress was alleviated. I added that that did not mean there was nothing to be angry about. That it worked out so well was, of course, very gratifying, but the relief he felt was independent of the outcome.

The patient said he had tried the same frank approach with his boss, telling Roger that they should be open about their feelings. Roger agreed but acknowledged that he found it very difficult to do. At a staff meeting shortly thereafter, Roger forgot that Grant was part of the conference and ordered sandwiches only for himself and the other participants. When Mr. Rausen called attention to the error, Roger told him not to take it personally and criticized him for being too sensitive. I tried once again to analogize from the past to the present: To be forgotten is painful for all of us, but given his chronic experience of being left out in childhood, it was understandable that this oversight would have ever so much more meaning for him. Mr. Rausen thought I was agreeing with Roger and telling him he was too sensitive. I had to extricate myself from the flypaper of his misunderstanding as best I could.

During one session Mr. Rausen sat forward in his chair, eager to show me an evaluation by his colleagues after a weekend seminar in which he had participated. Each member of the group was asked to fill out a questionnaire evaluating the other participants, as well as himself or herself, in terms of their respective contributions to the mission of the workshop. This document would prove to me, he felt, that he was well liked and respected and therefore not to be blamed for his predicament. But when I looked at it, I found that the summary of the evaluation others made of him was again essentially negative. As usual, he was given credit for hard work and dedication; these were the points he focused on as he showed me the document. He was uniformly criticized, however, for his unceasing craving for attention and approbation and for his inability to subordinate himself to the demands of the task and the team's goals. When I, as gently as I could, pointed out my impression that the evaluation was far from commendatory, he did not seem to hear me. Instead, he voiced his belief that Roger was trying to squeeze him out, rather than telling him what more he could do to prove himself. I suggested that he might feel that way here also: I was telling him that his colleagues' perception of him was indicative of a problem, but I could not tell him what to do about it. He gave me a look of incomprehension and talked about other, neutral matters.

In subsequent sessions Mr. Rausen continued to be impervious to self-examination. He knew he was doing a good job and would let no one take that away from him. He questioned whether he would continue with me in therapy. His sponsor at AA not only listened to him but had more advice for him. When I asked what his discussion with his sponsor had led him to think about and what advice he had been given, Mr. Rausen was unable to tell me anything specific. Rather than continuing in therapy and trying to make a go of it at his company, he thought he would instead look for another position: "When a guy is against you, there's nothing I can do except look elsewhere."

SESSION 10

There was a week's hiatus while Mr. Rausen attended an important meeting in another city. Initially, Roger had planned to go himself, but when other demands prevented him from leaving the office, he delegated Mr. Rausen to go in his stead. I saw the patient on the first day he returned to Chicago. He thought that he had handled himself well at the meeting. I asked him what this trip was all about and what he had learned from it.

Mr. Rausen had not lost the capacity to shock me with his inability to use words to create a meaningful whole. He spent fifteen minutes describing first the building in which the meeting took place and then how he got off on the wrong floor and wandered about looking for the conference room. He had to explain how he came to make this mistake and how angry he was at the person who had given him misleading directions. He began to describe his reaction when, having eventually found the correct room, he saw that whereas he was dressed in a business suit, as he felt one should be under such circumstances, others were dressed much more casually. Here I interrupted him.

THERAPIST: Is this what you are planning to say to Roger when you report to him?

MR. RAUSEN: Yes, I think so.

THERAPIST: (*Incredulous*) Really? Why would Roger want to know that you had a hard time finding the room?

MR. RAUSEN: I think it's important to set the stage. All these things influenced how I felt about the meeting.

THERAPIST: I really don't think Roger gives a damn about how you feel.

MR. RAUSEN: I'm a person . . .

THERAPIST: (*Interrupting*) No, you're not. At this meeting you were a pair of extra eyes and ears for Roger.

MR. RAUSEN: (*Taken aback*) I don't understand . . .

THERAPIST: Wasn't Roger going to go himself?

MR. RAUSEN: Yes.

THERAPIST: What did he want to find out?

MR. RAUSEN: How much they were going to raise the cost of their product and whether there was any room for negotiation.

THERAPIST: And did you find out?

MR. RAUSEN: (*In an aggressive, defensive tone*) I sure did. They're screwing us, and now they know that I know it. And they'll back down when we call 'em on it.

THERAPIST: Well, good for you. Isn't that what Roger wants to know?

MR. RAUSEN: Sure.

THERAPIST: Why not tell him that at the outset: Mission accomplished. You're a hero.

MR. RAUSEN: But that comes at the end.

THERAPIST: Exactly. And that's probably all he wants and needs to know. Or was there anything else of substance that happened?

MR. RAUSEN: I'm not sure; there might be a couple of things.

THERAPIST: You're not sure?

MR. RAUSEN: I guess not. No.

THERAPIST: Haven't you written out a report? An outline of the points you want to make?

MR. RAUSEN: No. Should I?

THERAPIST: When is the meeting with Roger?

MR. RAUSEN: This afternoon.

THERAPIST: You're not really prepared, are you?

MR. RAUSEN: What should I do?

THERAPIST: Well, in your place, I would call Roger and postpone the meeting. I'd be up-front; I'd say I'm just not prepared yet and would like some more time to pull my thoughts together. Then I would go home tonight and go over my notes, keeping Roger in mind—putting myself in *his* place. Not "What do *I* want from him?" but "What does he want from *me*? If I were Roger, what would I want to know?" That's what I would write down on a piece of paper. That would be my report. If it took more than one sheet of paper on one side, I'd start over and boil it down till I could tell him what I learned in ten minutes or less.

During this last interchange, Mr. Rausen had taken out his pen and was writing busily in his notebook.

I think it was here that it first became clear to me that his need for validation and his inability to obtain it were at the root of the incompetence that had put his job at risk. My attempts to connect his past history with his present search for love and approval had failed to influence his decision making. In this session I chose to alter my approach and force reliance by using the opportunity he gave me to enter the developmental spiral on the level of behavior. My belief that I had a better understanding of Mr. Rausen's developmental issues— that is, I was now oriented—let me intrude dramatically into his life. I know I really felt sorry for him. He truly did perform well, just as he always said he did, and I really hoped that he would not once again have to undermine himself with a counterproductive attempt to gain validation. Here was a situation, like Mr. Cain's, in which I was not dealing in retrospect with a failure whose significance he could deny and/or blame on someone else but with a disaster that was about to happen. Rather than simply orienting him, I also moved on to the next step in problem solving—the acquisition of skills—and gave him a concrete, helpful suggestion as to how he could achieve competence.

By helping him to reorient himself in his job situation, my suggestion met a mature selfobject need, namely, to restore a functioning self. At the same time, by putting myself into the position of the father who really cared what happened to him, I was also meeting what I considered to be the patient's implicit archaic selfobject need. His relationships with his superior in the army and his previous manager had shown that he could accept advice and turn it to good use. My hope was that if he used my suggestion and was able to satisfy Roger, the demonstration of competence might give him a necessary tool with which to adapt successfully. He had shown that in an environment in which he was "son" to an interested "father" he felt comfortable, could function well, and could grow. In his present situation, however, his manager seemed to have problems similar to his, namely, an affective block and the consequent inability to use empathy to make the relationship work. The long-term limited goal that I formulated during this exchange was to give him a sense of security in the handling of relationships, which perhaps could, in due time, make him feel safe enough to let his emotional life expand. My immediate aim was to give him the wherewithal to break the vicious cycle that had been set up between himself and Roger, so that his present situation would become tenable.

Mr. Rausen's need for reliance first came into our relationship when, after I had confronted him with his counterproductive behavior, he asked, "What should I do?" We had taken an important step; he now had some inkling that he needed help and a glimmer of hope that I might be able to supply it. I was careful to validate what deserved to be validated, emphasizing that though he was going about planning his report to Roger in a self-defeating manner, basically he had done a fine job; he was a "hero," his "mission accomplished." I could only hope that he heard me. In retrospect it seemed to me that he had been coming to see me, his notebook always in hand, waiting to extract and squirrel away the parental guidance he needed to manage things better. His taking notes at the end of this session indicated to me that something had happened between us that made sense to him. A positive transference, albeit a very limited one, was in place.

SESSION 11

> MR. RAUSEN: I want to thank you for last week. You've taught me that it's better to say that you're not prepared and want some time to think things through.
>
> THERAPIST: (*Inwardly dismayed by the patient's continued incomprehension and controlling the urge to strangle him*) How did it go?
>
> MR. RAUSEN: Very well. I did what you told me—thought of him and not of me. I must have told him what he wanted to hear, because he was very complimentary. He said he could not have done better.
>
> THERAPIST: How long did your meeting with Roger last?
>
> MR. RAUSEN: We had a half hour scheduled, but I was done in five or ten minutes. The rest of the time we just talked about things in general. He seemed real pleased.
>
> THERAPIST: And that is the result you wanted, isn't it?

MR. RAUSEN: It's the first time he was appreciative. I don't know why—I always work hard and I work smart. I just want credit for doing a good job. I haven't changed.

THERAPIST: Oh, yes, you have. How you go about getting that credit has changed. It's the difference between ramming your head against a brick wall and finding the door that will let you through. That door is called "empathy." By putting yourself in Roger's shoes and focusing on what the boss needs, instead of on what you want and feel you're entitled to, you ended up ahead of the game.

MR. RAUSEN: Maybe *he's* changed.

THERAPIST: Go back to the old way, and find out. Instead of focusing on what he needs from you, let him know how hard you work and why he should be more appreciative of you. You'll get your head handed to you once again.

Although the patient still did not seem to have grasped the concept, he was able to put my suggestions to good use. What had happened gave us an experience that could be referred to, a base for future discussion.

It seemed that Mr. Rausen's difficulty was in the attachment sector of development. He was concerned with validation because he did not have the confidence that he could recruit it. But a patient's need for validation cannot be met by the therapist's reassuring him that he is a worthwhile person, however well meant that reassurance may be. Validation needs to be directed at specific aspects of performance that truly impress the therapist as genuine achievements; only then is the therapist's emotional tone such that it makes a significant difference to the patient. From infancy on, we all understand on some level the difference between sincere and deserved approbation and empty compliments and meaningless reassurances.

Realizing that Mr. Rausen was seriously deficient in promoting attachment, I stressed autonomy and intervened on the behavioral level of the developmental spiral to help him gain competence. I expected—as in fact happened—that he would be validated by a pleasantly surprised Roger. That positive experience would enhance his self-esteem, and he would learn from it, as he had in the past. From the cognitive side he could master a technique for understanding another's needs, even though his lack of kinship and the consequent damage to emotional maturation prevented him from attaining genuine empathy.

MR. RAUSEN: He's complaining about something else now.

THERAPIST: What happened?

MR. RAUSEN: A letter went out that had a typo in it. I didn't proofread it before I signed it. When Roger saw the copy, he hit the ceiling and chewed me out. But it was the secretary's fault.

THERAPIST: But you signed it; it was your letter.

MR. RAUSEN: I don't get praised for all the letters that I sign that don't have mistakes in them.

THERAPIST: They probably figure that that's what you're paid for.

MR. RAUSEN: Bill (*his manager before Roger*) was different; he was always positive. He saw the good, not only the problem.

THERAPIST: You were lucky, just as with your superior in the army. These people were interested in you as an individual over and above your role in the organization, but you can't count on that kind of treatment all the time.

MR. RAUSEN: What do you think I should do?

THERAPIST: About what?

MR. RAUSEN: About this letter. He's pretty mad.

THERAPIST: Would you like to turn a minus into a plus?

MR. RAUSEN: How? The letter was sent.

THERAPIST: Well, if you had caught the secretary's mistake and pointed it out to her, what would *you* consider to be an appropriate response on *her* part?

MR. RAUSEN: I guess to say she was sorry and correct it.

THERAPIST: And maybe that she would be more careful in the future?

MR. RAUSEN: I've never had any of 'em say that. They try to make you feel stupid for calling attention to the problem that they've caused.

THERAPIST: Exactly. By disputing the validity of your complaint, they try to shame you. Doesn't feel good, does it?

MR. RAUSEN: No.

THERAPIST: I think you'd feel a lot better about a secretary who responded reasonably and apologetically and learned from her mistakes, rather than one who argued that it wasn't her fault or something.

MR. RAUSEN: Sure.

THERAPIST: So, turn it around and put yourself in Roger's place. He called you on a mistake. What do you think he should hear from *you?*

MR. RAUSEN: I got it.

THERAPIST: Okay, good.

I noted a definite change in Mr. Rausen's demeanor. He was less defensive and seemed to accept that I was able to help him. One swallow does not make a summer, but I believed there was an undeniable modicum of reliance in Mr. Rausen's "What do you think I should do?" Therefore, as the last exchange of the session indicated, he could now let himself understand what I was saying.

It can also be seen here that the patient was making strides in the area of autonomy. Of course the sectors of development that I have isolated for didactic purposes are not rigidly compartmentalized; they overlap. There was no doubt in my mind that Mr. Rausen's sense of attachment to me had also grown as I was able to demonstrate my usefulness to him, even though he did not seem to be particularly conscious of what was going on. I was very encouraged when, after I had made a comparison between his relationship to his secretary and his boss's relationship to him, he replied, "I got it."

Notice that I did not then ask him to clarify what it was that he "got." Did he really understand what I was trying to tell him? Certainly my history with him could cast some reasonable doubt on that. Nevertheless, there comes a time in therapy when it is more important to show one's confidence in the patient's growth and not act like an anxious parent trying to make sure that a child is really looking both ways when crossing the street. To strengthen the patient's justified increased confidence in his ability to cope with his problem, it was better to become more of a partner with Mr. Rausen rather than the wise uncle who always knows best.

SESSION 12

MR. RAUSEN: Roger said, "I'm pleased with all you are doing."

THERAPIST: Tell me about it.

MR. RAUSEN: I told him I was sorry, that I should not have let a letter go out with mistakes in it, especially to someone so important; it doesn't make the company look good. I said I appreciated being alerted to the problem so I could be more careful in the future. He smiled and responded by telling me that he knew the secretaries are getting increasingly careless and it aggravates him, too; it makes for a lot of unnecessary work for all of us.

THERAPIST: So, you see, by putting yourself in his shoes, thinking about him rather than yourself, you ended up on the winning side.

MR. RAUSEN: I was standing at his desk when I told him I was sorry. I was ready to leave, but he had me sit down so we could talk about other things. That's when he said he was pleased with what I was doing.

THERAPIST: Good. It worked out—the minus became a plus. In retrospect, do you think Roger was wrong to criticize you? In his position, what would you have done?

MR. RAUSEN: I guess I would have said something, but I wouldn't have blown my top.

THERAPIST: No argument, your way is the better way. But since Roger is your boss, it behooves you to work around the situation, which is what you're doing. He won't treat you the way you want to be treated, so you treat him the way he needs to be treated and, what do you know, you end up getting what you want.

MR. RAUSEN: It seems too easy.

THERAPIST: Once you know what to do, things are a lot easier.

MR. RAUSEN: I should have been able to figure this out for myself.

THERAPIST: I think you would have if shame had not stood in your way. When one has grown up, as you've told me you did, in an atmosphere where fault-finding and ridicule are used to enforce discipline, it's pretty hard not to be defensive. One is constantly preoccupied with trying to prove to people that one is not worthless, even when that is no longer an issue.

MR. RAUSEN: That's what AA did for me. They showed me I'm not worthless.

THERAPIST: Yes, and now you have to learn to believe it. Or at least act as if you believed it until you convince yourself that it's true. A couple of weeks ago, when we talked about that out-of-town meeting, all that prologue about how hard you had to work to find the room, and how you were dressed businesslike when others were not, was your way of saying, "See, I'm not worthless, I don't deserve to be shamed." But that's no longer the issue. Roger is not your father, whose respect and affection you wanted and could not get.

MR. RAUSEN: He acts like it.

THERAPIST: Not any more.

MR. RAUSEN: He sure did, though.

THERAPIST: As you demonstrated, how he reacts to you is under your control, at least to a great extent.

MR. RAUSEN: You mean it's my fault.

THERAPIST: There you go—now prepared to be shamed by me, when all the time I'm thinking of how well you are doing.

MR. RAUSEN: Everything is a fight.

THERAPIST: You can end a tug-of-war by letting go of the rope. When Roger criticized you for sending out the uncorrected letter, he was all set to get an argument from you. When you responded like a worthwhile, self-respecting person who is not afraid to admit he made a mistake, instead of shaming you he responded with relief and reciprocal generosity of spirit.

MR. RAUSEN: Maybe we're making too big a deal out of this. It was only a letter.

THERAPIST: No, this is a big deal. The occasional crisis or drama in a person's life is the exception. Usually we're engaged in a constant flow of everyday transactions that, in and of themselves, don't seem particularly momentous, but there is a constant, usually unspoken undercurrent of "Will my self-esteem be enhanced or diminished in or by this interchange?" Self-esteem is always being put on the line to some extent. The cashier who does not say "Thank you" when you pay your bill has a different effect on you than the one who does. And if you were thanked, was it pro forma or genuine, and so on. The only question is, How free are you to manage these situations as giver and as receiver? By apologizing to Roger for the flawed letter, you acknowledged his position and your responsibility to him as your manager. There was no defensive, self-serving attempt at argument on your part. Roger's self-esteem and sense of competence were not challenged—quite the contrary—and so he was free to see you and your contribution in a positive light and, in turn, extend his best self to you.

MR. RAUSEN: Is there anything I can read about that?

THERAPIST: Yes. (*Giving him a copy of* Understanding Psychotherapy)
Look it over, and see if it helps.

This session was a second turning point in the therapy. Now the
patient's capacity to rely on me—his trust that he would be helped
and supported by me in his struggle for competence—seemed to be
securely in place. As is often the case, once he was able to become
reoriented to his situation and develop appropriate coping mechanisms to deal with it, he showed a tendency to denigrate what had
been accomplished. "I should have been able to figure this out for
myself" or "I should have been able to do this long ago" are typical
statements made at that time. At this juncture it is important to give
the validation the patient is unconsciously seeking.

It was now possible to review past sessions with Mr. Rausen and to
look at his failures and contrast them with his present successes. This
sort of review, with an explanation for what was going on before, is
meant to reinforce the patient's coping capacity, as well as to promote
the ability to reflect on what it is that happened and what is happening now. In other words, it lets the patient gain insight into the developmental process, allowing an objective view of what the patient is
subjectively experiencing. Presenting Mr. Rausen with a copy of my
book was meant to acknowledge his growth and the sense that we
were partners in this therapeutic endeavor. It was also directed at the
sector of attachment. He understandably had difficulties in that area,
and it might be easier for him—that is, less shame-provoking—to
learn indirectly rather than directly from me.

SESSION 13

MR. RAUSEN: The stuff on shame really hit home.

THERAPIST: You recognized yourself?

MR. RAUSEN: The wanting so much to be liked, and that sick feeling
when you know you've messed it up again.

THERAPIST: But remember, you're not alone.

MR. RAUSEN: Is everybody that way?

THERAPIST: Until proven otherwise. You won't go wrong in that
assumption.

We went on to talk about the need to face one's own fear of being shamed, so that one can go beyond it and assess the other person's hopes, expectations, and concerns before deciding one's course of action. Mr. Rausen now volunteered many examples from his own childhood that confirmed how he had become so shame-prone and how that had interfered with the search for competence. He now understood why his colleagues had labeled him self-serving in the workshop questionnaire; his desperate attempt to show he was a "good boy" who deserved approval did not let him relax sufficiently to be a team player who took others' needs into consideration.

SESSIONS 14–17

As Mr. Rausen was able to function more empathically, people in the organization whom he had experienced previously as being unfriendly included him and took him into their confidence. He learned that his peers also regarded Roger as arrogant, overly demanding, and ungiving. But, as he said, "That's his problem, not mine."

"Not anymore it isn't," I commented. "It was your problem as long as you viewed yourself as a hapless victim; that has changed."

Yes, he said, he and Roger were getting along real well. Several times Roger had told him that what he was doing was "fantastic," and where previously Roger had avoided him, he now sought him out to talk things over.

Mr. Rausen assured me that he was keeping others' needs in mind and effectively managing various interpersonal situations. He applied what he had learned to his relationship with his lover and found that they were having a much better time together.

He asked to skip several weeks of sessions, because business commitments were becoming more demanding of his time. When he came back, he said that he was continuing to be successful in applying the things we had talked about. Roger had given a report of Mr. Rausen's progress to the vice president, and apparently it was a glowing one, for she had adjusted his salary upward and in a subsequent interview told him that the job was his as long as he wanted it.

Mr. Rausen now told me that he no longer needed psychotherapy and would stop. I agreed that he had accomplished what he came to do but suggested that he might want to come in once every two or three months so that we could monitor his situation. Mr. Rausen declined my suggestion; if he needed to come in he would call. And so we ended. He has not called.

CHOOSING THE APPROPRIATE INTERVENTION

Difficult cases are usually more instructive than those that go smoothly, and Mr. Rausen's situation was certainly not an easy one to deal with. We are taught to refrain from intervening until we are clear about what it is we are trying to accomplish and we believe that the patient is ready to hear what we have to say. In practice it is often not so easy to refrain from rushing in and trying to be helpful, especially when extraneous limits are placed on therapy. Premature attempts to intervene are at best useless, however, and at worst they just complicate matters.

I thought I understood that Mr. Rausen's inability to communicate meaningfully about his work situation was a reaction to the loss of his former manager. His new boss, Roger, did not lend himself to the role of guide and teacher, and the patient panicked. But my initial efforts to deal with this problem by connecting childhood deprivations to present circumstances failed, and I had to bide my time until I could assume the role of mentor.

What happened then illustrates once again how futile it is to break psychotherapy up into dynamic, cognitive, and behavioral forms. Occasionally it does happen that one modality carries the day; in Mrs. Willingham's case, a cognitive approach—helping her to clarify and focus her thinking—was enough to enable her to make the crucial decisions that altered her behavior and promoted competent functioning, and Mr. Dale required only a clarification of his affective dynamics to put significant change into motion. More often than not, however, efficacious therapy uses all three approaches in appropriate combination. In Mr. Rausen's case the opportunity for behavioral intervention presented itself, and I took it. His history had already shown me that he was most amenable to that sort of help. But once he had applied what I had taught him to good effect, it was possible to go over what had happened and explain why this behavior was successful; in this way I reinforced the experience cognitively. And with his self-esteem restored by Roger's validation of his competence, it was possible to make some dynamic inroads. He could now let himself understand the connections between his early experience and his present vulnerability to shame.

The therapeutic result with this patient was in many respects limited. Nevertheless, given his deep-seated characterologic problems and my initial pessimism as to whether anything could be accomplished with such a damaged and unresponsive person, I was more than satisfied. Looking back on my experience with Mr. Rausen, I am struck not only by what happened to the patient but by what happened to me as I worked with him. The developmental model, of course, applies to therapists as well as to our patients. In my case, I saw myself quite incompetent initially, and this threat to my sense of self-worth as a therapist led to some initial irritation. My realization that I would have to be content to struggle to orient myself to this patient's case, taking as much time as that required before attempting to do anything else, was helpful. Not until the tenth session did I feel I had achieved this goal, when my theoretical stance and clinical experience let me address his difficulty. I could then further reflect on the situation and, in appropriate narrative form, let him participate in my thoughts about his condition.

I have always found it very helpful to think about what is happening to me and what I am doing in terms of the developmental model. Such firsthand experience in finding oneself in one's own theory makes it that much more a comfortable and flexible therapeutic tool.

WILLIAM SEMIC

William Semic's internist referred him to me several months before the patient himself made an appointment. When Mr. Semic came into the office, his face was almost as gray as his suit. His slumped posture and dragging gait conveyed a sense of defeat. Fifty-two years of age, he looked older.

Mr. Semic made it clear that he had never been in a psychiatrist's office before and that he was very uncomfortable with this visit. He had come, he said, over his objections, and only because he had repeatedly been told to do so by his family doctor. He had initially consulted his internist because lately he was sleeping poorly, felt that he lacked his accustomed zest, and no longer looked forward to going to work. His doctor told him he was depressed and prescribed anti-depressant medications that had not helped him. He did not think of himself as sick but confused. For some time, he said, he had been considering resigning from his law firm, even though he was only fifty-two years old. He now looked directly at me for the first time and, in a challenging tone, asked whether I thought I could make up his mind for him. I replied that I would not presume to try to do any such thing, but that if I could help him to sort out the pros and cons of such an important decision I would be glad to do so. However, I added, before I could be of any help, I would have to know more about him generally, as well as about his work specifically.

Mr. Semic's facial expression conveyed that I had confirmed his suspicion that his visit to me was pointless, but he went on to give me more of the background of his present quandary. For many years, he had enjoyed an excellent reputation in his profession, but then he had failed to remain current with changes in the tax law that were making his work more complex. He should have gone back to school and done graduate work in taxation or accounting, but he had not done so; and as a result, he found himself with decreasing responsibility in his firm. Last year, he had had a coronary bypass operation, complicated by a postoperative infection, and was out of the office for two months. When he came back, his work had been shifted to others. For the better part of a year he had really had nothing to do, and it was clear to him that his partners wanted him to resign. He was not sure that he was ready to make that move, but he felt that the pressure on him to do so was mounting. He added, by way of confirming his ability to function, that he had totally recovered from his bypass and its complications and did not feel physically impaired. Here he ceased to talk, obviously waiting for my response.

As I listened to Mr. Semic, he did not strike me as clinically depressed; he seemed uncomfortable, unsettled. He came across to me as irritable, but I did not know if his mood was the result of having come to see me or had a deeper cause. Since he seemed to have no more to say, I asked him to tell me more about himself and his past and present relationships, to paint a picture for me that would let me understand better how he came to be who he is. Mr. Semic said he did not know what I wanted to hear about him. "Why not begin at the beginning?" I suggested.

Bill Semic was his parents' third and last child; his brothers were four years and two years older. In one of his mother's frequent rages, she told him—he was about ten years old—that she had seriously considered aborting her pregnancy with him. His mother had divorced his father almost immediately after his birth. She remarried when he was five years old, but he never got along with his stepfather; neither did his brothers. Family finances were marginal, and throughout his childhood there were continual arguments about money. As soon as he could support himself, Bill moved out. He now did not talk to either his mother or his stepfather. There would be no point to it, he felt, and he experienced no need to see them. Contact with his older brothers was limited; they were friendly but not intimate. Neither brother finished college and both were marginally employed.

Bill had impressed the local priest as bright and promising, and with this man's help he received scholarships and eventually became a lawyer. Although he remained on good terms with his mentor till the man died, he had long ago ceased practicing his religion. He married outside his church. His wife of twenty-eight years was not demonstrative, and he had always felt deprived sexually by her. Intercourse was infrequent and unimaginative. He was occasionally tempted to have an extramarital affair, but he dismissed these opportunities as more trouble than they were worth. A number of his partners were having or had had affairs, and as far as he could tell, such involvements brought nothing but problems. In spite of his disappointment in his sexual life, he valued his marriage and never considered divorce. He and his wife did many things together and enjoyed each other's company. They both liked travel, gardening, movies, and plays. They were friendly with a few other couples.

Jill, their daughter, was their only child; his wife had to have a hysterectomy shortly after the baby was born. Two years earlier, Jill married a ne'er-do-well against their wishes. "Now we're both down in the dumps about that," he added.

At the end of the session, I told Mr. Semic that I felt I did not yet have a thorough enough grasp of his problem and suggested we meet again. When he found that I had no specific advice to give him, he was clearly disappointed. He said he would think about coming back, but at this time would not make another appointment.

Mr. Semic was uncomfortable when he arrived, and I was uncomfortable when he left. It usually does not bother me if, after the first session, I am still in the dark about what is troubling a patient and what my role in that person's life is to be. An orientation—albeit provisional—is fundamental for therapeutic intervention, and, as in Mr. Rausen's situation, for example, it can take a while to get there. In the analysis of a psychoneurotic patient, it can take years. So it was not my lack of understanding as to how I might be of help to Mr. Semic that bothered me. Nor would I have been upset with myself if I had done what I thought was right and the patient refused to accept my recommendation to meet again; I am used to that as well. Here, however, I had not done what I should have done, and I had good reason to be troubled. Mr. Semic had clearly begun to delineate an area of incompetence in the autonomy sector of development. He described himself as an attorney who had looked forward to going to work but who—by his own admission—had not done what he should have done to maintain professional competence. This discrepancy did not make sense, and I should have focused on it and learned how it came to be reconciled in the patient's mind. I did not really know anything about the nature of the patient's work. That he was a lawyer apparently involved in tax matters was not nearly specific enough information to allow me to think knowledgeably about what he might tell me about his occupational difficulties. What sort of work did he actually do? Did he appear before the Internal Revenue Service? Was he involved in mergers and acquisitions? Or what? I knew no more about that at the end of the session than when he first walked into my office. How many partners did he have? What were the signals that led him to believe his partners wanted his resignation? Had he talked to anyone about his perception?

Often, as many of the previous cases illustrate, potential patients come in with no realization that their problems are related to some significant incompetence that is undermining the cohesion of the self, and we need to focus them on what needs to be further clarified. Mr. Semic, however, presented himself wearing the spiral of development on his sleeve. He had been declared incompetent and was faced with a decision that threatened to undermine his self-respect, namely, whether or not to resign from his firm. What did I do? I diverted the patient into a historical recital that, though it gave me many interesting facts about his development in the attachment sector, was therapeutically useless in view of the fact that his problem seemed to be located in the autonomy sector.

How did I get myself into this mess? Applying the retrospectoscope and putting the best face on it that I could, I decided that what got me off track was Mr. Semic's demonstrated lack of confidence in what I might be able to do with and for him. Without reliance, any intervention I might have made would have been useless, so I went on a fishing expedition to see why this deficit was there. I ended up no smarter than I had been before. Indeed, his childhood had been difficult, to say the least, but it had not prevented him from relying on his priest and now on his wife. If I had done what I should have done and usually do—namely, shown him by my questioning that I really wanted to know the particulars of his situation and to build for myself as accurate a picture as I possibly could of his view of his present dilemma—he would probably have mobilized his capacity for reliance, however limited, and something always comes of that.

As it turned out, I was luckier than I deserved to be. Mr. Semic called me three weeks after our initial session and made another appointment. He looked better to me this time than he had at first. He told me that the managing partner of his firm had told him he had been voted out and would have to leave at the end of the year. Yet his voice did not sound particularly distressed or angry as he spoke.

THERAPIST: How do you feel about what happened?

MR. SEMIC: In a way it's a relief, an end to uncertainty. I'm a glass-half-full person; I'll land on my feet.

THERAPIST: How will you do that?

MR. SEMIC: Now I'll have time to do some things I've always wanted to do. Maybe I'll go back for classes in literature and art. I've always wanted to study that and never had the time.

THERAPIST: Sounds good. What about money? How will this affect your life-style?

MR. SEMIC: No change. I'm in good shape. I've made good investments. I found I've always understood the market, and it's been good to me. The way I had it planned, I was going to retire at fifty-five anyway. I just need a few years of income to cover my living expenses, and then I'm in the clear.

THERAPIST: And how do you plan to do that?

Now some information surfaced that should have—and could have—but had not come out in the first session. When Mr. Semic first returned to work after his illness, the managing partner had talked with him and said that since there was not enough work to justify a partner's income for him, he should cash in his shares and work for the firm by the hour as a consultant; there was an aspect of estate planning in which his expertise was still needed and welcome. The suggested arrangement had actually seemed ideal to Mr. Semic; he would have an income, would not feel useless, and would still have time for other things. When he had confided this plan to his best friend at the firm, however, his friend had said, "Bill, tell them to go to hell! Why should you, after all these years as a partner, demean yourself by becoming an employee? They don't want you, so let them know you don't want them."

I now inquired about his colleague. It turned out that this man had long had a grudge against the partnership, feeling he should have had a leadership role that he was never given. I suggested to the patient that his friend was assuming that Bill felt as he himself did and was essentially telling him to make the decision he would make if he were in Bill's place. We then established that Bill did not share these sentiments and that his problem was not anger at his partners but some anxiety about relinquishing income before he was absolutely sure it was safe to do so. As he explained, he tended to be overly cautious, knowing that he could rely on no one but himself to provide. The arrangement suggested would suit him, but, he asked, would he be demeaning himself by taking it, as his friend suggested? I said emphatically that it did not seem that way at all to me; I thought of it as a business deal. "So do I," said Mr. Semic. When he left the session, he smiled genuinely for the first time and (reminding me of Mr. Dale) shook my hand vigorously. "I'm real pleased," he said.

In the third session, Mr. Semic showed no sign of stress, anxiety, or depression. He had accepted the arrangement suggested to him, and he proudly recounted how he prevailed when he insisted on being paid an hourly rate considerably greater than the customary rate for consultants. He felt that we had now accomplished what he had come for; he reiterated how good he felt about himself and our work. I agreed with his decision, and we parted company.

Although it took three sessions to accomplish what might have been done in two, the outcome was satisfactory. But my initial misstep continued to nag at me. I think I must have assumed that Mr. Semic's difficulties had to stem from his partners' jaundiced view of his contribution. In so doing I had mistakenly imposed onto the patient the feelings I would have had in similar circumstances. But that assumption was totally unjustified, as it usually is. He did have a self-esteem issue, but it was externally rather than internally imposed. His decision to accept hourly employment was a perfectly competent one, accommodating him to the environment and at the same time meeting his needs. It was only his friend's subjective view that he would necessarily lose face that gave him pause. When Mr. Semic came to me, he knew what he wanted to do, and once he was helped to articulate his decision and the background against which it was formed, only validation was needed to relieve his distress.

Fortunately, he came back to see me and gave me the opportunity to correct my error. When kinship is not a problem, a therapist's interest and willingness to help usually mobilize sufficient reliance to let the patient continue or, as in Bill Semic's case, to return, even when the therapist is in error. More often than not, our patients will give us another chance, and another chance after that, and then yet another, hoping to be heard and understood. The relationship between therapist and patient does not by itself constitute psychotherapy, however. It is not enough to be there for the patient in the relationship; one has to know what to say that will effectively address the patient's specific issues. Guided by a viable theory that is based on our ever-expanding knowledge of normal psychological development, we can organize what we hear in such a way that brief therapy will meet the patient's need appropriately and effectively.

CHAPTER 9

Restoring the Status Quo: Nadine Nelson and Gerald Shellman

F OR SOME PATIENTS, the value of short-term therapy seems to lie more in restoring the status quo than in altering for the better their way of attaining competence. The limitations of such a goal are not easy for the therapist to accept, but curbing our therapeutic ambitions offers us some comfort when the patient makes a unilateral decision to end treatment.

NADINE NELSON

Nadine Nelson, a thirty-seven-year-old stockbroker, consulted me when she was confronted by a number of personal losses: Her father had died recently, the woman who had recruited and trained her for her present position had been diagnosed with terminal heart disease, and a longstanding love affair was breaking up. Actually, she said, her lover had advised her for years to seek therapy, but she had resisted the idea. A fingernail-biter, a binge-eater, a compulsive worker, perfectionistic and seemingly unable to relax, she too realized that there was something wrong, but she had always resented the idea of therapy and found a host of pretexts to avoid treatment. Now she came only because the tension she was experiencing was interfering with her sleep, and she feared that her decision making at work would be impaired.

Ms. Nelson's tone was challenging, asking me to prove to her that therapy had something to offer. I answered her questions honestly, saying that other people in similar straits had benefited from therapy and that given her cooperation, I saw no reason why she too should not do so. Her lack of reaction to what I said, however, and her continuing doubts about the potential efficacy of a therapy that had barely gotten started indicated to me that Ms. Nelson's need for assistance was not matched by a readiness to engage me in a relationship that might supply it. Indeed, as I learned, the concept of a relationship in the sense of a mutual affective commitment was foreign to her. What she wanted was a prescription for dealing with different kinds of loss, and I do not think she ever accepted the idea that I was not in a position to give her such directives. She went along only reluctantly with my attempts at coming to know her as a person rather than telling her what to do.

It sounded to me as if Ms. Nelson's capacity for kinship was impaired, that her off-putting attitude was meant to protect her from intimacy that she could not handle. I therefore anticipated that her ability to rely on me for the help she needed would be a problem. Surprisingly, her childhood seemed to be a quite reasonable one. I had expected to hear a story similar to Mr. Dale's or Mr. Rausen's, in which parental incomprehension of a child's need for understanding and responsiveness had led to a defensive distancing and mistrust. But in Ms. Nelson's case, even as a child the patient had held herself aloof and avoided invitations to intimacy. Obviously I could not be sure, but her affective poverty made me think about the research suggesting that temperament is an inherited mental set. I tried hard to engage the patient in something beyond fact-finding, but to no avail. At the end of a session with her, I often felt foolish; it was similar to continuing to try to make friends with someone who is clearly not interested. This is not to say that nothing happened. Over a period of seven weekly sessions, Ms. Nelson sorted out the issues confronting her. She emphasized that it was *she* and not I who was finding the answers, however, and she routinely questioned her continued attendance at our sessions.

The patient told me that her father's death had in itself not perturbed her very much; what upset her was that she, an only child, was now responsible for her mother's welfare. Having to cope with her mother's mourning and helplessness in practical matters was a burden that Ms. Nelson found onerous. I tried to make dynamic hay out of the contrast between her mother's inability to manage her life and her own high functioning and the possibility that her fear of anything resembling a dependent relationship stemmed from associating dependence with helplessness, but my attempts failed miserably.

Ms. Nelson felt much better when she had arranged for her mother to move into the home of a distant relative who was willing to have the widow live with her as long as Ms. Nelson paid for her mother's upkeep. The patient's lover left their apartment during this time, and she found that she actually enjoyed the freedom to come and go as she pleased. She was sleeping much better and was no longer taking the soporifics prescribed by her internist. What was most upsetting for the patient was now her mentor's fatal illness and imminent death. Ms. Nelson relied on this woman as she never had on anyone else; perhaps this reliance was possible for her because the two women seemed to be characterologically very similar to each other. What affected Ms. Nelson most, however, was not the sadness of anticipated loss but the disorganizing effect her colleague's illness was having on her life. The daily conversations over breakfast or lunch, in which the two planned the investment strategies for various clients, talked about the politics of the firm, and discussed the influence of world events on their business, had been the axis around which her life was organized, and she missed them. I suggested that she might feel lonely for her colleague, but that turned out not to be the issue. It became clear to me that it was the support her mentor supplied that was important, not her person. As the days and weeks passed, Ms. Nelson's anxiety dissipated as she found herself functioning effectively on her own. Though she faithfully continued her visits to her dying colleague in the hospital, I could see her distancing herself from what was happening there.

As she was leaving at the end of her seventh session, Ms. Nelson turned at the door and asked, "Well, do I know enough about myself?" I was taken aback by the unexpected question, given her lack of interest in pursuing that task, and I answered, more bluntly than I would have if I had had some warning, "No, I think there is a great deal we have yet to learn." She smiled enigmatically and left. Her secretary called my office to cancel the next weekly appointment, and in that fashion Ms. Nelson ended her treatment.

The course of this therapy highlighted for me how much we as therapists count on the often-unspoken positive transference; without its enabling presence, our work loses much of the zest and excitement that both parties experience in the treatment process. In retrospect, it seems to me that the therapeutic relationship offered Ms. Nelson not intimacy, which she could not handle comfortably, but rather help at a distance, which was all she could tolerate. For her, therapy was a relationship without commitment that could be used to steady herself as familiar landmarks in her life were disappearing. It gave her time to demonstrate to herself that her manner of coping with life was still effective. Paradoxically, it seemed to me, she had come to therapy to prove to herself that she did not need another person in her life, that she could continue to function essentially alone.

In terms of the developmental model, it seems that early on, and for reasons unknown to us, Ms. Nelson suffered a severe deficit in the attachment sector of development. As many infants and children endowed with very high intelligence do, she compensated in the sectors of autonomy and creativity. Her relationships, such as they were—with her mentor, with me, and I suspect with her lover—met selfobject functions pure and simple. From each of her associations she derived what she needed in order to function autonomously. Not surprisingly, her affective armamentarium was significantly limited. Throughout our brief interaction I noted no depth or intensity of affect, whether positive or negative. Rather, there seemed to be an ongoing evaluation of whether or not she felt safe in her functioning—that is, whether or not she was competent to carry on on her own. Once I oriented her to the source of her distress and she was reassured on this point, she was less frightened by the impending loss. In other words, her sense of cohesion was now independent of the attachment to her mentor; personal relationships seemed to play no part in her sense of self-worth. Her capacity to right herself was honed to a fine point. Quick to use my clarifications to orient herself, she was able to develop the necessary coping skills and learned to rely on her private reflections exclusively. It seemed to me that our work together served her as a bridge to a more comfortable isolation.

GERALD SHELLMAN

Gerald Shellman, a thirty-two-year-old businessman, came to therapy with the complaint that in spite of a happy marriage and a good work situation he felt strangely tense and did not know what to do about that feeling. Inwardly, I was skeptical. If everything was so great, what was he doing here? But as I reviewed his past and present life situation, it did seem as if there was nothing significantly amiss that would have alerted me to the need for therapeutic intervention. He was functioning competently in the various sectors of development and seemed to enjoy the rewards of his efforts. The relationship with his wife and children showed him to be capable of participating successfully in relationships, and he did not flee from intimacy. Nevertheless, I had the distinct impression—although not as strongly as with Ms. Nelson—that he was keeping me at a distance. As he told me about his life, my interest and occasional comment did not bring us closer together, as is more often the case. I was at a loss as to what the immediate goal of our sessions might be and wondered whether the problem was so deeply buried that I might have to suggest that we use a psychoanalytic approach to fathom it.

In our third interview, Mr. Shellman found himself talking about his college days and a class reunion that he had recently attended. He then realized that he had not mentioned what was perhaps the most terrible event he had ever witnessed. During his senior year, a group of townies had invaded a party in his fraternity house; an argument ensued, and without any warning one of the trespassers pulled out a pistol and fired, killing Gerald's best friend. As he recounted this story, the patient was visibly shaken. I expressed the shock I too felt at hearing of this event, and we talked not only about the effect that the loss of his friend had had on him but about how the unexpected nature of the assault made it particularly overwhelming. I believed, judging from Mr. Shellman's reaction in the session, that we had come closer together in the telling of this gruesome tale and that a new phase of therapy could now begin.

In the next session, Mr. Shellman began where we had left off, going into more detail about the shooting and its aftermath. The college administration had suggested that those who had witnessed the event should avail themselves of the counseling service available at the university's health center. My patient did so, in addition to participating in group meetings arranged to help with the collective mourning of the student body. He felt that with the assistance of the psychiatrist, with whom he had several sessions before going home for Easter vacation, he had come to grips with his feelings about this tragedy. He did not return to the psychiatrist after school resumed. I reminded him that we were meeting in the month of April and that Easter had fallen on the previous Sunday. He responded as if he had been wakened out of a dream; it was obvious that this was the first time he had put two and two together and realized that the previous session, in which he had told me about the murder of his friend, had taken place on the anniversary of the killing. It turned out that every year for the past ten years, in the weeks before Easter, he found himself in a psychiatrist's office recounting the same story he had told me. He never went back to the same therapist, beginning anew each year and after Easter discontinuing treatment until the anniversary of the trauma once more approached.

I could see what was happening, and I pointed out the cycle that was leaving the underlying trauma unresolved. Each year he would, so to speak, attempt to park the memory with a psychiatrist, just as he had tried to do originally, only to find twelve months later that he had not rid himself of it after all. I suggested that here was the cause of his tension; it would not let itself be left behind but needed to be worked through. He agreed in principle but begged off making another appointment with the usual pressure-of-business excuse. I do not know whether he really registered my explanation that he was now falling into the same predictable pattern as he had every year and why it would be important to break that pattern. In any case, I did not hear from him again. I was quite sure that next year, during the weeks before Easter, he would again be moved by some vague discomfort to seek out a psychiatrist with whom, once again and to his surprise, he would relive the gruesome event of his friend's death.

LEAVING A DEFENSE IN PLACE

Mr. Shellman's attempt to deal with psychologic shock through dissociation had resulted in a post-traumatic stress disorder (Fishman 1989; Horowitz 1988; Shore 1986). The dissociated traumatic experience was apparently of such enormity that his participation in it, albeit only as a horrified onlooker, had put him beyond the pale of kinship as far as that sequestered memory went. Judging from his life story, he had the capacity for reliance that would have made further therapy possible. In his defensive isolation, however, he used his therapeutic contact to reinforce temporarily the dissociation of the experience from consciousness rather than to pursue its significance for his psychological life. Like Ms. Nelson, he could only allow himself to form an archaic selfobject relationship with a psychiatrist whose interest and attention permitted him to let established coping mechanisms reintegrate his sense of self once more (Gardner 1991). Of course, at some future date, under different circumstances and perhaps with a different therapist, the necessary integration of the trauma Mr. Shellman had suffered might still take place.

Should I have called Mr. Shellman when I did not hear from him for a few weeks and try to get him to resume therapy? I decided against it. I thought he was telling me as convincingly as he could that at least for the time being, he could do no more. That does not mean that in either Ms. Nelson's or Mr. Shellman's case nothing was accomplished. Short-term therapy lends itself very well to helping patients regain their equilibrium so that they can again use their competencies to the best advantage. Our frustration that they may be left with painful or unnecessarily confining limitations is something all of us have to learn to live with in this profession.

CHAPTER 10

Problem Solving: Roger Povalente

ROGER POVALENTE

THANKS TO THE architect's miscalculation, my waiting room is small to begin with, and Roger Povalente's size only accentuated its stingy dimensions. As he rose from his chair, I anticipated that his head would hit the ceiling. Actually, he was probably only about 6 foot 5 inches tall, enough to dwarf me but not all that unusual in today's young men. What made him look so enormous—indeed, menacing—was the tension that emanated from his body. As his short-sleeved shirt and tight jeans made evident, his muscles were very well developed and seemed to be in a permanently contracted state. His furrowed brow, the intense stare of his icy blue eyes, and the constant clenching and unclenching of his fists conveyed an impression of barely controlled rage. And when we began to talk, it turned out that he was every bit as angry as he looked.

Mr. Povalente, twenty-seven years old, was unhappy to find himself in my office and made it clear that he had no confidence that I could help him; he regretted having listened to an acquaintance, one of my former patients, who had suggested that he come to see me. A college graduate, he seemed to be quite intelligent, but he had held only menial or semiskilled jobs, and usually for only short periods of time. Most of our session was taken up with his angry cursing, as he complained about the supervisors on various jobs he had held: No one seemed to want to give him a chance to prove himself, everybody else made mistakes and got away with it, but he was fired as soon as he did anything that gave even the shakiest ground for dismissal. He wanted to go back to college and obtain an advanced degree in computer science, but in his rapid cycling through jobs he could not save the money needed for further education. His parents, he said, had gotten "fed up" with him; they not only did not assist him financially but had barred the door of their house against him. (He ignored my query about what had led to this estrangement.)

All this was told to me in a belligerent tone of voice that had the undertone of suspicion typical of the paranoid personality. When I drew the session to a close, he was quick to tell me that I had done nothing for him, but in the same breath—and somewhat to my dismay—he asked for the time of his next appointment. In retrospect I can now appreciate that this patient must have aroused significant anxiety in me. Otherwise I would have appreciated that his asking for another appointment indicated he was ready to rely on me for help. No matter what else may be playing itself out, that readiness is the essential indicator that therapy has a chance of succeeding.

Rather than becoming more comfortable with him when we met the next week and the weeks thereafter, I felt both more alienated from him and more uncomfortable. In his eyes, it seemed to me, I was becoming identified with the establishment and those who not only would not let him share in the good things of life but took pleasure in his misery. I learned that he had a black belt in one of the martial arts, was (as I supposed the moment I saw him) a bodybuilder, and had met my former patient at the target range where he practiced pistol shooting. To say the least, this information did nothing to reassure me.

After our third appointment I found myself feeling increasingly unsafe in the presence of this bundle of rage, who could, I felt, lose control at any moment and hurt or even kill me. I would have liked nothing better than to part ways with Roger Povalente, but I feared that if I took him up on his oft-repeated complaint that I was not helping him, a suggestion that we end our visits might well be the last straw in his history of failures and bring about the very attack that I wanted to preclude. I felt I had a tiger by the tail.

As the day of our next scheduled appointment drew closer, my unconscious presented me with a memory from a book I used to read to my children in their preschool years. It was a story about a gentle giant who, by his sheer size and occasional clumsiness, alarmed the population and was banished from one village after another. He managed to make friends with a little princess who was not frightened by him, however, and she persuaded her father, the king, to let him visit the castle and play with her. I recalled the line "When it was hot he blew a gentle breeze"; as I remembered it, there was a picture of his huge face looming over the castle as he air-conditioned it for the comfort of the royal family. My next thought was "But he never hurt anyone." I now understood that this chain of unbidden associations was related to Roger Povalente. The fear he had inspired in me had obscured the fact that, in spite of all his rage, his height and strength, and his air of impulsiveness, he had never harmed anyone. Although he felt he had been dismissed unfairly from one position after another, he had wreaked no vengeance but had meekly gone on to the next job and to the one after that. He had no history of fighting or brawling. What he manifested was a nasty vocabulary and a menacing appearance.

Of course, what I felt to be my insight into Roger's situation affected my way of dealing with him in our next session. Believing I had oriented myself and reached a level of competence vis-à-vis his situation, I was much more decisive in organizing our transaction. Instead of letting him ramble on about the "lousy deal" life had dealt him, I directed the discussion to what was going on in his present job in the warehouse of a department store. Clearly hired for his size and brawn, he loaded and unloaded trucks with such items as refrigerators and stoves. As always, having been on the job for several months, he sensed that his foreman and his fellow stock clerks were taking sides against him. Furiously he gave voice to threats like "I'll kill that asshole" or "One of these days I'm going to pound that fucking son-of-a-bitch's head in the sand." I asked, "Is this the way you talk at work?" Another series of expletives and invectives followed; the gist was that, pushed to labor without letup at this always difficult and sometimes dangerous job, he believed he had every right and reason to vent his feelings as he saw fit and toward whomever he chose.

At this point, I could have validated him in that it did indeed sound as if he was being taken advantage of, but I chose not to do so. Instead, I disagreed with his justification for his angry outbursts, saying, "I could talk that way, but you may not." This got his attention. I went on to explain that if I were to speak in such a foul-mouthed, menacing manner, people would be offended but nobody would take it seriously. Just looking at me, they would see that such talk from me was empty bluster; I could not do much damage to anyone. But anger coming from him, especially if accompanied by physical threats, could not help but be taken seriously. He could not afford that sort of language unless he truly meant to strike terror into his listeners. That, I pointed out to him, was why he kept getting fired. We all would get frustrated if we were similarly used and abused, but what would be a meaningless expression of dissatisfaction from anyone else was seen as a threat of real danger when it came from him. As a result, the only thing his employers wanted between themselves and him was distance. "You are a tall, powerfully built man who is obviously in superb physical shape. With your angry look, and sitting there like a coiled spring, you scare me—even though now that I know you better I also know that violence is not your style," I said. Here, I offset my confronting him with his incompetence in interpersonal relationships by validating the legitimacy of his distress in the work situation.

Roger was very surprised at what I had said. Because he thought of himself as helpless and put upon, it had never occurred to him that he might appear otherwise. What he heard me say apparently made an impact, for the next time we met he was able to talk in more reasonable terms. A lot of things made better sense to him now. He had never looked at himself as I had. I acknowledged that that was hard to do and said that was why I felt the most helpful thing I could do for him was to hold up a mirror in which he might see himself as others saw him. He reported that following our talk he had modified his behavior and had calmed down at work. He thought he could salvage the situation. The job paid well, and if he could stay there, he would be able to save toward his goal. As the session was drawing to a close, he said that he had gotten what he came for and did not want to make another appointment. I encouraged him to continue to apply what he had learned about himself, and we said good-bye. At the end of the month I sent him a bill for my services; no check arrived, and I was glad just to let the matter drop.

I was startled when, some four months later, I opened my office door to see Roger Povalente once again seated in my otherwise empty waiting room. Though he was dressed much more neatly than he had been previously—he was wearing khaki pants, a clean white shirt, and a double-breasted blue blazer—his face still had the sinister, contemptuous sneer with which I was familiar. His expression did not change when he saw me. "Hello, Doctor," he said, drawing out the words and making them seem more like a threat than a greeting. As he spoke, his right hand traveled in a deliberate arc across his chest and into his jacket. All I remember of that moment is my surprise at finding myself so inwardly calm as I saw his hand reaching toward his shoulder holster. I realized that I had underestimated his paranoid potential and that this might be the end. "I came to bring you your money," he grumbled, pulling out an envelope instead of the revolver that I had expected. I thanked him and was about to invite him to come into the inner office for a few minutes, but sensing what I was about to do, he waved me off and opened the door to the hall. As he left he tossed over his shoulder, "I'm back in school," and disappeared down the stairwell.

COMPENSATING FOR A DEFICIT IN KINSHIP

A patient's anger does not ordinarily bother me; on the contrary, openly expressed affect, whether positive or negative, is easier to deal with than affect that is concealed. Furthermore, Roger Povalente was certainly not the first angry man I had treated who also happened to be tall and burly. The immediate discomfort I felt on meeting him had nothing to do with either his anger or his size. What made me anxious was the unabated sense of alienation, the absence of the unspoken but usually present sense of kinship between human beings. There was never the feeling of "we" that usually develops as the patient becomes aware of being understood by the therapist. Ordinarily the therapist and patient share the belief that, in principle at least, people can be of help to each other. As two human beings, no matter how different we may be in many respects, we share a commonality that we can both draw upon as we work to find a modus vivendi. Even Ms. Nelson and Mr. Shellman, in spite of their limited capacity for reliance, manifested that bond. It is a rude awakening when someone like Mr.

Povalente comes along and shows us that this is not always the case.

Once the significance of the kinship need is recognized, however, the patient whose difficulties lie in that area can be better understood. In essence, such a person is saying that far from being helpful, human transactions are a source of stress. The prospect of a therapeutic relationship not only does not offer hope but further compounds the specific problem that brought the patient to therapy.

It is crucial for the therapist to control the anxiety that this sort of situation may generate and step back to look at the assets the patient has brought to the treatment. Mr. Povalente not only had good intelligence but had been able to harness it and graduate from college. He had not acted on his anger, and he had withstood the trauma of being banished from his parental home. So there was something to work with; what was blocked was the approach to treatment to which we are accustomed. We are ready to understand and meet a patient's need for attachment, for reliance and validation, and thereby build a basis for helping the patient—through clarification, education, and interpretation—toward resolutions that will let the person function more competently. With patients like Mr. Povalente, however, who feel safer in isolation but are driven to seek help under the stress of their circumstances, an orientation to the immediate problem and a direct and directive approach are very effective in making the most of whatever capacity for reliance they have been able to mobilize.

Since I saw Roger Povalente, many years ago, I have had a good number of patients like him who benefited from suggestions to alter their ways of attempting to cope. Though affectively handicapped and lacking in the attachment sector of development, they have made the most of their cognitive abilities and are quick to learn and to adapt. Usually the suggested change relieves an interpersonal friction that, because of their affective deficit, they were unable to see, much less resolve. When it comes to the more basic issue, the inability to trust people, we find ourselves in a catch-22. To do our work we need a modicum of trust, and that is precisely the deficit that needs to be addressed with these patients. Nevertheless, the cognitive correction that such a patient has been able to accept is not necessarily a makeshift; quite the contrary, in many cases—as seems to have happened with Roger Povalente—I have seen it make a significant difference in helping a person achieve a higher level of functioning and a correspondingly improved sense of self-worth.

The issue that needed to be addressed in Mr. Povalente's case was his inability to understand or benefit from the affective communication that is essential for social adaptation. The damage, from the developmental point of view, lay in the affective portion of the affect/reason sector. I think it is quite likely that his mind-set rose out of the isolation he experienced as he had to accommodate to a world whose most important messages he either misunderstood or missed entirely. He was chronically affectively disabled, but because no visible handicap announced his condition, no allowances were made for him, no rehabilitation had been instituted, and he found himself pushed more and more out of the mainstream.

Kinship problems manifested by gross deficiencies in the area of affective communication are by no means limited to patients who present a paranoid or paranoid-like defensive posture. Like all our patients, people with kinship problems seek therapy when the order they have managed to establish threatens to unravel. Under that pressure they are capable of hearing and integrating what they would ordinarily dismiss. The hope, of course, is that the successful implementation of the therapist's clarification will, over time, lead to experiences that mitigate the patient's isolation and permit a sense of kinship with the human race to develop. In any case, it has been my experience that patients so basically alienated from the human condition do not stay in therapy once they have gotten what they came for. Serious affect deficits can be therapeutically corrected, as was shown by Mr. Dale. In my experience, however, the patients amenable to such therapeutic construction or reconstruction seem not to have been deprived of kinship but to have been made ashamed of their affective needs later in development, when they turned to their parents for validation of those needs.

The patients discussed in the last three chapters are usually classified with diagnostic labels that describe the pathologic aspects of their personality, such as borderline, paranoid, inadequate, schizoid, or avoidant. These designators are usually attached to patients with significant impairment in the area of kinship and subsequent difficulties in affect management. In spite of the severity of their character pathology, however, brief psychotherapy can be very helpful to these patients. Indeed, it is often the only therapy that they can tolerate, given their difficulty in maintaining relationships that are not in some way destructive or self-defeating. As almost happened in the last case, it is easy to be blinded by the negative aspect of such patients' difficulties. Without overlooking their limitations, we must remain aware of the strengths that they have been able to develop in spite of their problems. By applying the developmental model we can help these patients to achieve competence and a sense of cohesiveness that they did not have prior to treatment.

References

Alexander, F. (1954). Some quantitative aspects of psychoanalytic technique. *Journal of the American Psychoanalytic Association, 2,* 685–701.

———— (1958). Unexplored areas in psychoanalytic theory and treatment, Part II. In *The scope of psychoanalysis* (pp. 319–335). New York: Basic Books.

Basch, M. F. (1980). *Doing psychotherapy.* New York: Basic Books.

———— (1983). Empathic understanding: A review of the concept and some theoretical considerations. *Journal of the American Psychoanalytic Association, 31,* 101–126.

———— (1986). How does analysis cure? An appreciation. *Psychoanalytic Inquiry, 6,* 403–428.

———— (1988). *Understanding psychotherapy: The science behind the art.* New York: Basic Books.

———— (1991). Are selfobjects the only objects? Implications for psychoanalytic technique. In A. Goldberg (Ed.). *Progress in self psychology,* Vol. 7 (pp. 3–15). Hillsdale, NJ: The Analytic Press.

———— (1992). *Practicing psychotherapy: A casebook.* New York: Basic Books.

———— (1994). The selfobject concept: Clinical implications. In A. Goldberg (Ed.). *Progress in self psychology,* Vol. 10 (pp. 1–7). Hillsdale, NJ: The Analytic Press.

Budman, S. H. (1981). *Forms of brief therapy.* New York: Guilford Press.

Burke, J., Jr., White, H., & Havens, L. (1979). Which short-term therapy? Matching patient and method. *Archives of General Psychiatry, 36* (Feb.), 177–186.

Crits-Christoph, P., & Barber, J. P. (1991). *Handbook of short-term dynamic psychotherapy.* New York: Basic Books.

Davanloo, H. (1980). *Short-term psychotherapy,* Vol. 1. New York: Jason Aronson.

Erikson, E. H. (1950). *Childhood and society.* New York: Norton.

Fishman, G. (1989). Psychoanalytic psychotherapy. In *Treatments of psychiatric disorders,* Vol. 2. Washington, DC: American Psychiatric Association.

Flegenheimer, W. F. (1982). *Techniques of brief psychotherapy.* New York: Jason Aronson.

Freud, S. (1912a). The dynamics of transference. In *Standard Edition,* Vol. 12 (pp. 97–108). London: Hogarth Press, 1958.

———— (1912b). Recommendations to physicians practising psycho-analysis. In *Standard Edition,* Vol. 12 (pp. 109–120). London: Hogarth Press, 1958.

———— (1913). On beginning the treatment. (Further recommendations on the technique of psycho-analysis, I). In *Standard Edition,* Vol. 12 (pp. 121–144). London: Hogarth Press, 1958.

———— (1914). Remembering, repeating and working-through. (Further recommendations on the technique of psycho-analysis, II). In *Standard Edition,* Vol. 12 (pp. 145–156). London: Hogarth Press, 1958.

———— (1915). Observations on transference love. (Further recommendations on the technique of psycho-analysis, III). In *Standard Edition,* Vol. 12 (pp. 157–171). London: Hogarth Press, 1958.

Gardner, J. R. (1991). The application of self-psychology to brief psychotherapy. *Psychoanalytic Psychology, 8,* 477–500.

Gay, P. (1988). *Freud: A life for our time.* New York: Norton.

Gedo, J. E. (1979). *Beyond interpretation.* New York: International Universities Press.

————— (1988). *The mind in disorder.* Hillsdale, NJ: The Analytic Press.

Goldberg, A. (1973). Psychotherapy of narcissistic injuries. *Archives of General Psychiatry, 28,* 722–726.

Goldberg, C. (1995). The analytic template: Help or hindrance in the conduct of psychotherapy? *Clinical Social Work Journal, 23,* 87–99.

Greenson, R. R. (1967). *The technique and practice of psychoanalysis,* Vol. 1. New York: International Universities Press.

Gustafson, J. (1984). An integration of brief dynamic psychotherapy. *American Journal of Psychiatry, 141,* 935–944.

Horowitz, M. (1988). *Introduction to psychodynamics.* New York: Basic Books.

Jones, E. (1953). *The life and work of Sigmund Freud,* Vol. 1. New York: Basic Books.

Karen, R. (1994). *Becoming attached.* New York: Warner Books.

Kohut, H. (1971). *The analysis of the self.* New York: International Universities Press.

————— (1977). *The restoration of the self.* New York: International Universities Press.

————— (1984). *How does analysis cure?* Chicago: The University of Chicago Press.

————— (1987). *The Kohut seminars.* Edited by M. Elson. New York: Norton.

Lazarus, A. A., & Fay, A. (1990). Brief psychotherapy: Tautology or oxymoron? In J. K. Zeig & S. G. Gilligan (Eds.). *Brief therapy* (pp. 36–46). New York: Brunner/Mazel.

Malan, D. H. (1976). *The frontier of brief psychotherapy.* New York: Plenum Medical Book Company.

Mann, J. (1973). *Time-limited psychotherapy.* Cambridge: Harvard University Press.

————— (1981). The core of time-limited psychotherapy: Time and the central issue. In S. H. Budman (Ed.). *Forms of brief therapy* (pp. 25–43). New York: Guilford Press.

Meltzoff, A. N. (1985). The roots of social and cognitive development: Models of man's original nature. In T. M. Field & N. A. Fox (Eds.). *Social perception in infants* (pp. 1–30). Norwood, NJ: Ablex Publishing Corporation.

————— (1990). Foundations for developing a concept of self: The role of imitation in relating self to other and the value of social mirroring, social modeling, and self practice in infancy. In D. Ciccetti &

M. Beeghly (Eds.). *The self in transition: Infancy to childhood* (pp. 139–164). Chicago: University of Chicago Press.

Nathanson, D. L. (Ed.). (1987). *The many faces of shame.* New York: Guilford Press.

———— (1992). *Shame and pride: Affect, sex, and the birth of the self.* New York: Norton.

———— (1994a). Shame, compassion, and the "borderline personality." *Psychiatric Clinics of North America, 17,* 785–810.

———— (1994b). The case against depression. *Bulletin of the Tomkins Institute, 1*(2), pp. 1–3.

Shore, J. (1986). *Disaster stress studies: New methods and findings.* Washington, DC: American Psychiatric Press.

Sifneos, P. E. (1992). *Short-term anxiety-provoking psychotherapy: A treatment manual.* New York: Basic Books.

Stern, D. (1985). *The interpersonal world of the infant.* New York: Basic Books.

———— (1989). Crib monologues from a psychoanalytic perspective. In K. Nelson (Ed.). *Narratives from the crib* (pp. 309–319). Cambridge: Harvard University Press.

———— (1990). *Diary of a baby.* New York: Basic Books.

Strupp, H. (1980a). Success and failure in time-limited psychotherapy. A systematic comparison of two cases: Comparison 1. *Archives of General Psychiatry, 37* (May), 595–603.

———— (1980b). Success and failure in time-limited psychotherapy. A systematic comparison of two cases: Comparison 2. *Archives of General Psychiatry, 37* (June), 708–716.

———— (1980c). Success and failure in time-limited psychotherapy. Further evidence (comparison 4). *Archives of General Psychiatry, 37* (Aug.), 947–954.

Tomkins, S. S. (1970). Affects as the primary motivational system. In M. B. Arnold (Ed.). *Feelings and emotions* (pp. 101–110). New York: Academic Press.

———— (1980). Affects as amplification: Some modification in theory. In R. Plutchik & H. Kellerman (Eds.). *Emotions: Theory, research and experience* (pp. 141–164). New York: Academic Press.

———— (1981). The quest for primary motives: Biography and autobiography of an idea. *Journal of Personality and Social Psychology, 41,* 306–329.

Waddington, C. H. (1966). *Principles of development and differentiation.* New York: Macmillan.

Zeig, G. K., & Gilligan, S. G. (Eds.) (1990). *Brief therapy: Myths, methods, and metaphors.* New York: Brunner/Mazel.

Index

Affect, deficit in, 54, 139, 175; ranges of, 18–19. *See also* Anger—rage; Contempt; Disgust; Distress—anguish; Enjoyment—joy; Fear—terror; Interest—excitement; Shame, and humiliation; Surprise—startle

Affect/cognition, 8

Affective commitment, lack of, 163, 165

Affective connections, 15. *See also* Problem-solving intervention, guide to

Affect/reason, 8–10; damage in, 175

Affect theory, *xxv*

Alcoholics Anonymous, 122, 136, 139, 140–41, 143

Alcoholism, 63, 74, 120, 135, 136, 137

Alexander, F., *xiii*, 71, 177

Anger—rage, 19; and shame, 96. *See also* Povalente, Roger

Anniversary of trauma, 166–68

Anxiety, and positive change, 102; provocation of, *xxii–xxiv*; of therapist, 170–71, 173–74

Arrested development, 54, 127

Attachment, 8–9, 47; and competence, 123; deficits in, 147, 165; problems in, *xxv–xxvi*

Autonomy, 8–9; as compensation, 165; and competence, 123, 147, 149

Avoidance, and shame, 80, 91

Barber, J. P., *xxii*, 178

Basch, M. F., *xv*, *xxii*, *xxv*, 8, 9, 10, 13, 14*n*, 29, 30, 46, 54, 55, 66, 67, 73, 125, 126, 127, 177

Boredom, 18

Brief psychotherapy: and anxiety provocation, *xxii–xxiv*; capacities of, *xiii*; and clarification and

Brief psychotherapy *(cont.)*
guidance, 131–55; compared with
psychoanalysis, 16–17; contraindi-
cations for, 120–27; and developmental deficit, 54–75; introduction
to, *xxi–xxvii*; models of, *xiii–xiv*;
and patient as change agent,
37–53; and patients' needs, *xi*; and
problem solving, 169–76; and
restoring self-esteem, 99–101; and
restoring status quo, 162–68; and
restricted access, *xii*; and shame,
77–98; and validating change,
102–19. *See also* Time-Limited
Psychotherapy
Budman, S. H., *xxii*, 177
Burke, J., Jr., *xxiii*, 177–78

Cain, Jacob, 76, 77–101, 145
Case studies, *xiv*. *See also* Clinical
examples and illustrations
Character change: correcting a
deficit, 54–75; and lengthier ther-
apy, 120–27; and patient as agent
of, 37–53; and restoring self-
esteem, 99–101; and shame,
77–98; validating, 102–19
Clarification, and brief psychother-
apy, 131–61
Clinical examples and illustrations:
Cain, Jacob, 76, 77–101, 145; Dale,
Warren, Jr., 29, 54–75, 98, 127, 135,
138, 139, 154, 160, 163, 175;
Furlong, Franklin, 102–19; Jerome,
Ralph, 18–34, 41, 43, 46, 54;
Longwood, Michelle, 120–27;
Nelson, Nadine, 162–66, 168, 173;
Povalente, Roger, 169–76; Rausen,
Grant, 131–55, 163; Semic,
William, 155–61; Shellman,
Gerald, 68*n*, 166–68, 173; Taft,
Denise, 3–17, 18, 19, 29, 31, 32, 33,
34, 41, 54; Willingham, Bea, 37–53,
54, 100–101

Cognition, 8–9. *See also* Affect/cog-
nition
Cohesive self, 24, 125
Communication, effective, 15. *See
also* Narrative; Problem-solving
intervention, guide to
Compass of shame, 80, 91. *See also*
Shame
Competence: and attachment, 123;
and behavioral discrepancy, 57;
and challenge to, 137, 138; and
meaning to patient, 16; restoring,
18–34; striving for, 10, 14*n*
Competence model, 10. *See also*
Developmental spiral
Contempt, 19
Countertransference, 56
Creativity, 8–10; as compensation,
165
Crits-Christoph, P., *xxii*, 178

Dale, Warren, Jr., 29, 54–75, 98, 127,
135, 138, 139, 154, 160, 163, 175
Davanloo, H., *xiii*, *xxi*, 178
Decision making, 46
Defense, leaving in place, 168
Dependence, and helplessness, 164
Depression, and development, 13;
signs of, 42
Development, sectors of, 8–10, 17
Developmental deficit, correcting,
54–75
Developmental model, *xiii–xv*; and
developmental spiral, 10–13, 17;
and focusing treatment, 3–17; and
goal setting, 3–17; and patient's
strengths, 7; and problem-solving
intervention, 14–15, 17; and
restoring competence, 18–34; and
sectors of development, 17
Developmental spiral, 10, 17; in
reverse, 24. *See also* Competence
model
Disgust, 19

Disorganization, 164; affective, 55; and shame, 79; and word salad, 134
Distress—anguish, 18–19, 40
Dynamic therapy, 17

Embarrassment, 67. *See also* Shame
Empathic immersion, 126
Empathic understanding, 73
Enjoyment—joy, 19
Erikson, E. H., 29, 178

Fay, A., *xxiv*, 179
Fear—terror, 19, 24
Feedback, 124
Fishman, G., 168, 178
Flegenheimer, W. F., *xxii, xxiii, xxiv*, 178
Freud, S., *xii, xiii, xxi, xxv–xxvi*, 29, 56, 68, 119, 125–26, 127, 178
Furlong, Franklin, 102–19

Gardner, J. R., 168, 178
Gay, P., 126, 178
Gedo, J. E., 68, 178
Gilligan, S. G., *xxii*, 180
Goal setting, 3–17, 50–53
Goldberg, A., *xxv*, 178
Goldberg, C., *xxi*, 178
Greenson, R. R., 29, 178
Guidance, 72; and brief psychotherapy, 131–61
Gustafson, J., *xxiii*, 179

Havens, L., *xxiii*, 177–78
Horowitz, M., 168, 179
Hypochondriasis, 20. *See also* Jerome, Ralph

Infant research, 30; and shame, 78, 92
Initiative, center of, 11, 13, 14
Interest—excitement, 19
Interpretation, 125

Intervention, appropriate, 154–55; and problem-solving, 14–15, 17, 125

Jerome, Ralph, 18–34, 41, 43, 46, 54
Jones, E., 126, 179

Karen, R., *xxv, xxvi*, 30, 179
Kinship, 30, 32; affirmation of, 109; compensating for deficit, 173–75. *See also* Selfobject transferences
Kohut, H., *xxv, xxvi*, 11, 24, 29–30, 46, 48, 55, 72, 126, 179

Lazarus, A. A., *xxiv*, 179
Longwood, Michelle, 120–27

Malan, D. H., *xiii, xxi*, 179
Mann, J., *xiii, xxi, xxiv*, 179
Mature selfobject, experience, *xxvi*; need, 145
Meltzoff, A. N., 30, 179
Mirroring, 72. *See also* Validation

Nacherziehung, 127
Narcissistic personality disorder, *xxv*, 55, 76
Narcissus, 76
Narrative, 40, 119. *See also* Communication, effective
Nathanson, D. L., *xxv*, 18, 19, 56, 77, 80, 179–80
Negative transference, *xxv*. *See also* Positive transference
Nelson, Nadine, 162–66, 168, 173
Nonerotic positive transference, *xxv–xxvi*. *See also* Positive transference

Oedipal conflict, *xxv*
Orientation, 15, 43; altered, 49–50; and clarifications, 166. *See also* Problem-solving intervention, guide to

Paranoid personality, and suspicion, 170

Positive transference: and attachment disorders, *xxvi*; components of, 30; and kinship, 30; and reliance, 30–32, 33; and therapeutic significance, *xxv*; and therapists' reliance on, 165; and validation, 30. *See also* Transference

Post-traumatic stress disorder, 168

Povalente, Roger, 169–76

Practicing Psychotherapy: A Casebook (Basch), 9

Problem-solving intervention, 14–15, 17, 125; and brief psychotherapy, 169–76; guide to, 14–15; staircase, 28

Progressive therapy, 17

Psychoanalysis, compared with brief psychotherapy, 16–17

Psychoneurosis, 126

Psychosexuality, 8–9

Psychotherapy: and developmental model, *xiii–xv*; dynamic, *xxi*, 125; insight, *xxi*; potential phases, 124–25; psychoanalytically oriented, *xxi*. *See also* Brief psychotherapy; Time-Limited Psychotherapy

Psychotropic drugs, 13, 51

Question of Lay Analysis, The (Freud), 119

Rausen, Grant, 131–55, 163

Reason. *See* Affect/reason

Reflection, 15. *See also* Problem-solving intervention, guide to

Regressive therapy, 17

Reliance, 30–32, 33; absence of, 159; capacity for, 40, 48, 135, 168; and mentor, 164; readiness for, 44, 170. *See also* Selfobject transferences

Rescue, need for, 43

Resistance, 125–26

Sadness, 18

Self-esteem, building, 99–101; and meaning to patient, 16; restoring, 99–101; and youth, 51

Selfobject experience, mature, *xxvi*

Selfobject transferences: alter ego, *xxvi*, 30; grandiose, *xxvi*; idealizing, *xxvi*, 30, 48; mirror, *xxvi*, 30; twinship, *xxvi*, 30. *See also* Kinship; Reliance; Validation

Self-righting tendency, 6, 11, 165–66

Semic, William, 155–61

Shame, 56, 77–98; and affective needs, 175; and anger, 96; compass of, 80, 91; as discipline, 134; and disorganization, 79; and humiliation, 19; as obstacle, 119

Shellman, Gerald, 68*n*, 166–68, 173

Shore, J., 168, 180

Sifneos, P. E., *xiii*, *xxi*, 180

Skills acquisition, 15. *See also* Problem-solving intervention, guide to

Stern, D., *xxv*, 30, 180

Strengths, of patients, *xiv*, 6–8, 11–16; and building self-esteem, 99–101

Strupp, H., *xxiii*, 180

Surprise—startle, 19, 172

Taft, Denise, 3–17, 18, 19, 29, 31, 32, 33, 34, 41, 54

Time-Limited Psychotherapy, *xxiv*. *See also* Brief psychotherapy

Tomkins, S. S., *xxv*, 18, 180

Transference, *see* Negative transference; Positive transference

Trauma, unresolved, 166–68

Unconscious, 56

Validating character change, 102–19
Validation, 30, 44, 48, 72, 124, 147, 172; and shaming, 94. *See also* Mirroring; Selfobject transferences
Violence, perceived threat, 170–73

Waddington, C. H., 6, 180
White, H., *xxiii*, 177–78

Wiedergutmachen, 75
Willingham, Bea, 37–53, 54, 100–101
Withdrawal, and shame, 80, 91
Word salad, 133–34

Zeig, G. K., *xxii*, 180